THE

SCANDAL

OF

SILENCE

THE
SCANDAL
OF
SILENCE

BY

EDWARD·M·KEATING

RANDOM HOUSE

NEW YORK

THIS BOOK IS DEDICATED TO THE

MEMORY OF

ANGELO GIUSEPPE RONCALLI

AND

THOMAS J. McKEON,

TWO SERVANTS OF GOD WHOSE LIVES

WERE SERMONS OF LOVE,

AND WHOSE DEATHS TOOK THEM TO GOD

CONTENTS

THE
SCANDAL
OF
SILENCE

1

THE NEW MAGI

WHETHER we like it or not, whether we are prepared for it or not, we are in the midst of a revolution. This is not the sort of revolution that is the child of a few agitated minds, this is not a revolution reinforced by guns and terror; this is an entirely different sort of revolution, one that has slipped up on us, like a thief in the night, and that threatens to transform the world at a rate far beyond our powers to forestall or accelerate. We are in the grip of something so elusive, so hidden, that from outward appearances there is nothing extraordinary going on at all. Indeed, many of us imagine that the current world is merely a continuation of all that has happened, a culmination of all that has gone before, and that beyond this moment the next will appear, quite properly fulfilling the ordinary promise contained in our present point in history. It is like counting numbers: ten always follows nine, and eleven always follows ten. This would be the ordinary expectation when one views history unfolding. The present revolution, however, is proceeding in exactly the opposite direction; it is revealing that, though time may progress in a single direction, not everything needs to follow suit. While in the ordinary process of counting ten does follow nine, we have a different sequence if we count backwards, in which case nine follows ten.

This is the nature of our present revolution. We wish to return to that point in history when Western civilization was united, to that moment just before Luther when there was still an opportunity to preserve our unity. Once the fracture of Christendom occurred, we rushed downhill to this moment, when we have to make our final decision on whether we are going to retrieve unity or continue our historical drive toward complete fragmentation. If we do the latter, it is only a matter of time until we enter into our final fragmentation, a fragmentation greatly accelerated by the forces of atomic energy let loose by our last will and testament. In this sense, we are on the brink of a great decision: either we tumble into a disastrous conclusion, or we draw back from the brink and somehow retrace our steps to that moment when we once had unity, thence to proceed through a new history in which that unity is preserved.

The last several centuries have witnessed two most significant contributions to our modern plight. They came one after the other. The first was the tendency of man to dethrone God, thereby making himself independent of any higher authority and thus assuming ultimate authority in all things. Interestingly enough, this act also released man from responsibility to another being. The second significant contribution, which occurred only when man had enthroned himself, was man's own efforts at dethronement (possibly *abdication* would be better). Man, now alone in his world, found it a very lonely place because all there was was *man*. That something greater which made life endurable was gone and man was left to his own devices, which proved very inadequate. And yet man sought to deceive himself by the process of creating an illusion of inevitable progress. This principle required that he fill this world with all sorts of things so that he might finally feel fulfilled himself. Possessions were symbols of faith, as if the more a man possessed the greater was his faith, and everyone felt that consummate faith would produce some sort of eternal reward—if only there were an eternity to grant reward.

The greatest possession man has ever had is the power to destroy. And we have that now in a final form. Man, in the greatest sense, is a god who can obliterate the world. And yet, man (god) has abdicated his throne, or at least he has tried to. For so long man pretended that he was irresponsible; now he knows better because he has the power of deciding the matter of universal life or death. From this he shrinks; he wishes to pass on this responsibility to someone else. And yet, who else is there to make the decision? As things stand, or rather, as they stood until most recently, there was no one; God was dethroned and man was doing his best to abdicate, which is just another way of saying that man was trying to run away from himself.

All this, of course, was based on an illusion, an illusion that man could determine whether or not God exists. The fault lay in the concept of dependence. God's existence isn't dependent upon man's determination; it is quite independent. On the other hand, man's existence is totally dependent upon God. This is the pivot on which all else turns. And it is on this pivot that men's minds are swinging toward the only alternative to their present plight.

Central to this pivotal change is the sudden disillusionment with division. However, to do away with the effects of division and to provide for unity require an awareness of a commonness that transcends the temporal. How, if there is nothing greater to allow a commonness among us all, can there be union between the American Democrat and the Russian Communist, between the rich and the poor, the good and the bad, the possessed and the dispossessed, the black and the white, the atomic powers and the nonatomic powers, the colonialist and the nationalist? We have worn our labels and each of us has claimed superiority over everyone else; we would be as gods. But this hasn't worked and we are searching for something that will.

Cynics belittle the religious revival of the postwar era. There are some who take great delight in seeing a slackening of interest or in pointing out that the revival is only skin deep and more a social action than a spiritual one. But these social commentators themselves go only skin deep in their analysis. They see only the surface, the temporality, without understanding that these very people whom they convict of shallowness or social aspirations could just as easily have formed another club. The significant thing is that they chose to orient themselves toward a spiritual organization, an organization which, regardless of profundity or efficacy, has as its prime purpose the bringing together of man and God. The extraordinary aspect of this is that *God* was finally assuming some significance in modern society.

Although this turning to religion has many flaws, it is nevertheless a critical reversal of recent tendencies and it is the thing that in time, God willing, will allow us to retrace our steps toward universal union.

What, then, is this universal union that can transcend differences? Quite simply, it is the union we share as children of God; under God's paternity we are brothers.

Of course, we have always had this paternity and this fraternity, but we lost sight of it for a very long time. We all—Catholics, Protestants, Jews, atheists, and everyone else—spent centuries seeing those from whom we were separated, for whatever reason, as alien. Because of our fear of the unknown, the different, the stranger, we saw only the persona presented to us; we all failed to pierce the façade, and thus we failed to see the *man*.

Division is inevitable. No two people are alike; neither are two ideas. Not all beliefs are correct, but neither are all alien beliefs in complete error. Thus are we divided. But division must never be allowed to form a breach in our love, a love not necessarily of an alien idea or belief but of him who holds that idea or belief. How can I, as a Catholic, profess to love God if I secretly (or even not secretly) hate a Prostestant or a Jew or an atheist or a Communist? If division must inevitably lead to hate (or its handmaiden, pride), then I say, let us do away with division. Let us break down the walls of separation, let us embrace each other as men, rather than remain divided and unloving.

The key is the human embrace, not necessarily an embrace of ideas. I may love my brother who recommends euthanasia, but I don't have to accept euthanasia as an addition to my store of beliefs. What is essential, of course, is that we learn to distinguish between the person and the belief. With the *person* we are united in brotherhood; from the belief we may be separated, but separated in charity. For example, do we love someone less because he suffers from cancer? We love him regardless of the cancer and we would separate him from the disease, not because we hate the disease but because we love him who suffers. This sort of illustration is relatively simple. But what of the alcoholic? Whereas cancer can strike anyone, isn't the alcoholic at least partly to blame for his condition? And if he is, shall we love him less? If we decide to, then we are judging him on his lovability, which is really only God's business, and God's business is quite uncluttered with such things; He loves the alcoholic just as much as He loves any of us.

What, then, of the Protestant, the Jew, the atheist? They are all the same: God loves everyone the same. What is really important is how we love God and how we love each other.

Actually, why should we seek union? In order that we may love. We don't now, we should all confess; not really. A few do—there are Catholics who love, there are Protestants who love, and others who love. And we must all love so that we may attain life everlasting. This is what it is all about. We must all perish at some moment, whether atomized or as quiet victims of old age, so death is common to us all. What is not common to us all is love, and this we must attain. This requires the union of brothers, not the separation of strangers.

What is said of society in general can also be said of the

Catholic Church. That is, the Church must be part of mankind's monumental effort to reverse the march of history to
inevitable disaster. The Church can no longer live its exclusive life, and those who comprise the Church can no
longer live separate lives, alienated from and suspicious
of the other.

The question naturally arises of whether the Church is
presently continuing in its traditional ways or whether significant changes are taking place. It is abundantly clear that
in terms of society in general the Church is going through a
revolutionary change. We have the clear evidence of the
present Vatican Council as well as the Church's growing
practice of cooperating with other Christians and with non-
Christians in an attempt to resolve so many problems that
plague our times.

More obscure, however, is the situation within the
Church itself. And this has to do with the relationship between the clergy and the laity. There appear to be two
schools of thought on this matter.

One school (composed almost exclusively of laymen)
maintains that prior and present clerical practices clearly
indicate the need for the clergy to revise their attitudes, to
cease being so authoritarian and paternal. This school, with
great justification, insists that the clergy must stop thinking
of the laity as simply pairs of hands and begin to realize that
lay minds have a great deal to offer the Church. The further
contention is that unless there is a change in clerical thinking, the Church faces the serious prospect of anticlericalism. All things being equal, this school would be entirely
correct. But all things are not equal.

The other school (needless to say, this one composed almost exclusively of clerics) says that there is nothing basically wrong between clergy and laity that won't be cured by finding something for the laity to do. But the adherents to this school are courting disaster if they think that laymen will be content merely to serve them as they have in the past.

I said above, however, that all things are not equal, even though at this time our traditional patterns of thought prevent us from seeing the true situation within the Church.

The great struggle within the Church has little to do with the clerical-lay relationship; the struggle is between the orthodoxy that has dominated the Church for over four hundred years and Christian heterodoxy (a term to be enlarged upon later). And ranged on the two sides of the issue are all Catholics, regardless of any other distinguishing mark.

There is a growing faction within the Church that seeks to advance toward accepting this Christian heterodoxy, and in this force are both lay and clerical Catholics. Opposing this is the group which prefers the traditional way of life, and this group is composed of both clergy and laity.

Possibly a personal reference will help us see the true lines of demarcation and not just the apparent. It involves the writing of this book. When I began the work, I was completely convinced of the justice of lay claims that laymen are pressed into an inferior status, that they are of little use to the clergy except to support their exorbitant way of life, and all that sort of thing. In constructing an argument that would send clerics reeling, I proposed to prove conclusively that the layman was just as good as the cleric, except that the cleric wouldn't admit it. This is really quite true if we look at it from the viewpoint of love—that is, I, as a layman, am capable of loving God just as much as any cleric—but, come to think of it, it does rather smack of pride.

The initial effort proved to be more of an emotional trial than an expository triumph, so I threw my original remarks away and began on a new tack that eventually led me to the same dead end. What drove me to the dead end was the fact that the higher I built the wall between clergy and laity, the more I began to realize that it was all nonsense. Every time I tried to lump all clerics into one group (a very bad sort, entirely) and all laity into another mutually exclusive group (a very decent sort, entirely), I always found someone like Hans Küng or Thomas Merton an embarrassment, or for that matter a number of priests in my own life who, I once found myself saying, were more laymen than I. And then, of course, there are scores of fellow laymen who think Vatican II some sort of subtle heresy brought about by Communists hiding behind a clerical front. I recall one such who was convinced that the Jesuits and the Communists were actually in a sinister conspiracy to take over the world. Finally, I was faced with the obvious inconsistency of my remarks with the planned dedication of this book, which was (and still is) to two clerics.

The error of my approach lay in my thinking in terms of labels and not of ideologies. This error we have begun to correct; we have begun by convening Vatican II and we have begun by ranging the forces of belief against contrary belief rather than ranging personas against each other.

It is quite obvious to anyone keeping score on Vatican II that an awesome revolution threatens to take place within the Church. Indeed, this current business is so utterly extraordinary I dare say that before it all began no one, particularly a layman, could possibly have imagined that the voting on critical schema would ever be so unbalanced as it has been. The popular press prefers to describe the two trends within the Church as the conservative and the liberal, with the latter having much the better of things. Unfortunately, these two terms, so thoroughly identified with political and social phenomena, have tended to obscure the Christian realities being expounded by the Council. I prefer to describe the situation as being a fundamental cleavage between those who prefer to preserve Catholic orthodoxy and those who prefer to originate a new principle that can best be described as Christian heterodoxy.

Catholic orthodoxy is a rigid state of mind that insists on the absolute speciality of all things Catholic, and that insists on total isolation from the contaminating influence of Protestantism and all other religious opinion; further, this orthodoxy is highly suspicious of modern ideas such as democracy and social justice, and feels comfortable only in the Catholic mental fortress erected at the Council of Trent.

In order to forestall any misunderstanding about the term *Christian heterodoxy,* let me begin by saying that I am not advocating that Catholic dogma and theological principles be dumped into some melting pot with every other sort of Christian idea and mixed into some witch's brew of the most common tastes. Rather, I use this term to describe the transcendence of Christian love over a particular orthodoxy, not only of belief but of practice as well. What most reveals our present state of Christian thought is the double awareness of denominational difference and of Christian unity. We within the Church have now reached a point in our history where we can appreciate the merit of our religious convictions while at the same time we can also appreciate the fact that vast numbers of our brothers believe other things. In brief, there is a growing faction within the Church that accepts Christian heterodoxy as a *fact,* and then goes beyond that to an awareness that this heterodoxy is possessed by those we love.

The conflict is between those who, for whatever reason, prefer to cling to the orthodoxy that flowed from the Council of Trent and those who have seen Trent as the great obstacle to love and wish to replace it with something better. And in this conflict we find that the traditional classifications of Catholics as *clergy* and *laity* are giving way to ideological ones. Vatican II makes the issue of ideologies clear; what is rather obscured is the question of the concurrence of those outside the Council with what occurs within. And it is here that I feel the Church is in for its most severe test. While it is very true that the Council Fathers are planning sweeping changes, what I fear is that these plans are going to run into the thick wall of attitudes that will do much to impede effective implementation. This wall, though including many lay attitudes, is built principally of clerical habits and prejudices.

It would be so easy to say that the vast majority of the

clergy are bent upon retaining the status quo out of some ill will toward the laity, as well as toward society in general. But honesty requires a deeper awareness of the situation, an awareness that brings us inevitably to the most serious and basic difficulty: the determinants of the Church's existence are now its authoritarian structure and its clerical primacy.

The Church works downward. Rome, whether through the person of a pope, the Curia, or a council, issues a particular proclamation that carries enormous weight, as it should. However, Rome must always percolate downwards through bishops to the parish level, and what once began as something precise and very clear becomes imprecise and quite muddied before it reaches its objective, the people. Bishops and priests are very variable, and what is readily understood and accepted by some is not so readily understood and accepted by others. For example, Rome has spoken on racism in a way that leaves absolutely no doubt, but certain Southern bishops have not quite the charity of Rome and they have employed very dubious practices to frustrate papal intentions. This sort of difficulty holds true about the principle of religious liberty, newly enunciated by Pope John; we scarcely expect Spanish bishops (and the Spanish state) to interpret this in the same way that German bishops do.

This percolation problem is inherent in any authoritarian system, and it is a constant menace when the charisma has been institutionalized. What was once mysteriously elusive, grandly transcendent, becomes something different when placed under human authority and subjected to human imperfection. Something is lost.

But more serious will be the problem of clerical primacy, the practice of placing the clergy in a position superior to the laity.

Not very long ago it would have been virtually impossible to find a strong sense of fraternity between clergy and laity. In those days, so newly gone, the priest and layman were quite alienated from each other because of the wall of separation based on their identities. And to a large extent, they still are. It is not exposing any secret to talk of the centuries-old and still widespread conceit of priests who feel quite elevated above the laity once their special vows set in. This, of course, is a very human failure, based on temporal rather than spiritual considerations.

It was once part and parcel of being a layman that he remained silent, passive, and obedient in all things. It was also inherent in the priestly state that one spoke to, for, and about the laity; that one was active in all aspects of Catholic life, whether one was supervising the local altar society or deciding social beliefs; and that one demanded obedience of those multitudes beneath oneself. The difficulty did not arise over sacramental or spiritual matters; it arose over temporal primacy. And to a great extent this difficulty is still with us.

Before we analyze temporal primacy and its burdensome consequences, just a few remarks are needed to lay bare the basis for the absence of criticism of spiritual primacy.

Spiritual primacy is in the order of things Catholic. Since Christ founded His Church on Peter, He founded it on the principle of authority from the top and not on the principle of permission from the bottom. This principle was necessary since it was God's rule that was to be brought down to earth and not man's up to God. The key, of course, was the need to preserve infallibility and holiness, qualities that God possesses and that man simply doesn't. Needless to say, infallibility would be restricted to faith and morals since any further extension would erode the principle of free will. God gave the Church the various sacraments, which, after the Ascension, would necessarily be administered by men. But not just any men—specifically designated men who would have to be signally distinct and identifiable and, through procedure, possessing the authority to administer the sacraments. Obviously, this could not be done by popular vote of those to receive the sacraments, but only by those whose commission stemmed from the original commission of Christ. This primacy doesn't end with the sacraments but extends to teaching. Yet, while the former offers no difficulties, since the sacramental power is so distinct and precise, the latter, depending on how far we extend the principle of teaching, is apt to produce problems, particularly in modern times.

Regardless of this reservation, there is no doubt about the need for spiritual primacy. However, sharp differences arise over the principle of temporal primacy, which originated not at the time of Christ's original commission but much later.

The difficulty in approaching the issue of temporal primacy lies in the problem of breaking through a whole mass of subtleties that bear upon lay-clerical relations and getting to the heart of the matter: attitude. It would be quite easy for a layman to set forth a litany of complaints which, taken individually, would appear peevish or too trivial for comment and which would thus lose the layman his clerical audience, whose attention he earnestly seeks.

Probably it would be best to revert to the point about attitude, and in so doing I would like to describe an incident that may serve to illustrate both the basis of the lay-clerical cleavage and the matter of primacy.

I recall some short time ago visiting with a seminarian who represented, to the layman's view, the great hope for the future. He was intelligent, having a tremendously inquiring mind. Over many months we had talked with great pleasure about such disparate subjects as theology, literature, politics, and psychology, as well as anything else that came to mind. He was deeply interested in the layman (he was in the anomalous position of being half-layman and half-priest, just having received his tonsure) and the future of the Church. This moment of recollection involved itself with lay participation in the Church, and I advanced the notion that lay businessmen could probably do a better job administering the affairs of the parish than the priest, and could also relieve the pastor for more directly pastoral activities. A number of us were present, and the idea was getting a thorough discussion when my young friend burst out, "You can say all you want about the layman doing this or that, but I certainly don't want any layman telling me how to run *my* church!"

There was a moment's frigid silence. We were all aware of my friend's intense embarrassment, arising out of the fact that his studied insistence over many months that laymen should function actively in the Church had suddenly been contradicted by this spontaneous outburst. Everyone present knew that the outburst was what he really believed.

"*My* church!"

Here is the heart of the matter. If anything could be said to divide the laity and the clergy, and further, if anything could be said to form the basis of anticlericalism, it is the fact that the attitudes exhibited by the great mass of the clergy reveal that they think—whether consciously or unconsciously—that they are the Church and that the laity are somehow related to the Church but not quite in it.

It's as if the layman were just outside the gates, generally inclining himself toward some formal entry, *ever so close, ever so inclined, ever so well intentioned,* but not quite inside the Church.

Theologically, the Church is the Mystical Body of Christ, whose membership consists of those baptized, in communion with Rome, and possessing faith. On this basis, a layman qualifies for membership in the Church equally with the clergy. The problem arises out of the development through history of what can only be described as a corporate structure composed of those who have taken certain vows that bring them into a particular relationship with the ultimate authority of the Church, the pope. Ranging down from the pope, we have the various bishops who, in turn, have under them the various individual priests who head the parishes. Along with all this personnel are the organizations needed to effectuate the spiritual and temporal policies of the pope and his central directive body, the Curia. This requires an enormous organization. In effect, the newly ordained priest becomes an employee of a vast and complex corporate structure which a recent study has revealed to be one of the two most efficient organizations in the world.

All this poses a difficult problem for both priest and layman. They belong to one community, the Mystical Body, but are separated by the existence of the corporate structure, which, though originally intended to function for the benefit of all, has tended to work to the detriment of the Mystical Body by rendering the Church into two bodies, one with power and identity and one without power or identity. Further, it separates the laity from the clergy because the cleric, who is in the corporate structure, tends to identify himself too exclusively with the structure and not enough with the rest of the Mystical Body as a whole. The results, particularly in modern times, have been disastrous, in terms of damage not only to interpersonal relations, which is bad enough, but also to the efforts of the Church in its earthly mission.

A moment ago I referred to the laity as being without power or identity. This point must be enlarged upon because it apparently causes considerable misunderstanding among both the laity and the clergy. To begin with, the laity have considerable power and identity in their secular as well as their spiritual lives. However, the difficulty of power and identity arises when we think of the laity vis-à-vis the corporate structure. The fact is that the layman has no desire to be a member of the corporate structure, in the sense that he does not seek the priestly role in life (since that is not his God-given vocation), although at times various laymen seek a more direct participation in the structure by entering the Catholic education system or some other department within the structure. But these are isolated cases that do not impinge on the present question (although they will be discussed later).

The problem of the relationship between the laity and the clergy, in this context, arises over the power and identity of the laity when considered in terms of the corporate structure. But this consideration *ipso facto* makes no sense: it is quite obvious that a layman doesn't and shouldn't have any power or identity vis-à-vis an organization he doesn't belong to. Just as nonsensical would it be for me to claim power or identity in terms of A.T.&T. if I neither work for nor have a proprietary interest in A.T.&T. Vis-à-vis both the Catholic corporate structure and the A.T.&T. corporate structure, I have but one form of power and identity: I am an outsider, a stranger.

However, both corporations are monopolies, and how they function does tend to affect my life. My phone bill may go up or my Church bills may go up. To such an extent I am involved. The key point about both corporate structures is that they exist for me; I don't exist for them. Because giant structures tend to think more of themselves than of those they should serve, we have the Public Utilities Commission to supervise A.T.&T., to make certain that *the company* serves *us*.

However, with the Church we have no such regulatory body; we must rely on the good will of those within the structure never to lose sight of the fact that they exist to serve us, never to assume that we exist to serve them. This is not to strain for sovereignty or exalted status; it is to ensure that the corporate structure doesn't have self-perpetuation as its goal but that it always aims to serve humanity and fulfill the earthly mission of the Church, which is the ultimate goal of the salvation of all souls and the more immediate one of preparing the way through corporal acts of mercy. That is why the pope is called "the servant of the servants of God."

And it is precisely because so many of the clergy fail to convey this impression that the laity complain about the corporate structure. In all candor, if most clerics knew the depth of lay feeling and, more sadly, the basis for it, they would first be shocked and then, hopefully, mortified.

When a priest is made a pastor, he takes command. Oh, I don't mean over such trivial and ordinary things as mass schedules and confessions; I am referring to the commanding attitude many a priest displays in virtually every connection. He commands a school; he commands a new church building. Notice that he doesn't suggest or ask for lay counsel, despite the fact that the laity are far more involved than he since they have the children and they must pay the bills. But in the end it is "Father's" new church and "Father's" new school. The pastor is served, by the ladies who decorate his altar and the parishioners who cut his hair or repair his rectory for less. Now, it is perfectly proper that those within a community should serve one another. Just as the pastor serves his parishioners, so should the parishioners serve their pastor—but *not* in such terms that the pastor assumes certain things as his due. The end of such a process is that the pastor may be tempted to believe that these services are his by right but eventually loses even the capacity to offer thanks for whatever courtesies and services are extended.

Again, this is not a condemnation of the individual clerics involved; it is a condemnation of the divisive situation arising out of a misconception of relationships. It is a matter of attitude, an attitude that has its origins in ancient history and its perpetuation in the slow erosion of the individual who is actually the victim of a system that confuses spiritual primacy with temporal primacy.

If anything, bishops are even more victimized by the system. While a pastor lives very much among the laity, a bishop lives in almost regal isolation, surrounded by clerics or near-clerics (by that I mean chosen laymen so involved with corporate matters that they lack only the vows to make them full members) who serve him and his policies. Whenever a bishop is outside his chancery, he is always on display, not only before Catholics but before society in general as well, which treats him with a mixture of deference and amusement as it takes in his ceremonial costume and that sort of thing. When a bishop enters the life of a layman, he generally appears as a distinguished visitor from some other place, rather like a head of state, say, from some new nation in Africa where really important people wear flowing robes and have a charming little hat perched on the back of their heads. It's all so very alien.

Because of temporal precedent established in an antiquated past, the bishop's person is rather aloof. If one wishes to approach, the better course of action is to genuflect and grace the episcopal ring with something vaguely resembling a quite common kiss. If one chooses to engage in some sort of colloquy with his excellency, one does so fully aware of the language barrier and also of the fact that the bishop seems just a bit vague in his attention, as if he were preoccupied with some grave matter of state—such as preparing for a subsequent engagement with a similar group of laymen. In the personal lives of the laity, the bishop is little more than an adornment, like the coat of arms one's family may hang on the wall of the study. Naturally, there is no personal contact. True, the personas may collide, but then only in the form of ritualized gestures and responses. One would scarcely rise above one's station to confront the bishop as mortal man.

Now, I dare say bishops don't like this any more than those who surround them, but there it is; history, that curse of humanity, has not only planted the seed of separation, but has seen to it that through the frailty of man it should flourish seemingly forever. Again, what promotes this separation is not spiritual primacy (which is actually a contradiction in terms, since our common spirituality serves as a bond) but temporal primacy, a terrible hangover from the past.

To repeat a point rather, there is no lay aspiration to *be* the bishop or to compete with him in any manner. What I am pointing out is the separation between us. The danger, as the layman sees it, is that bishops and to a certain extent the clergy in general will succumb to the temptation to take all of the trappings of office seriously. Unfortunately, we suspect too many have succumbed, so that rather than suffering from a sense of inadequacy for the serious and superior office conferred upon them, they take unwarranted pleasure in having so many people make so much fuss over them.

Then, too, there is the danger of power. Without presently analyzing the forces which have conspired to bring about the situation, we cannot deny the fact that bishops wield tremendous power in their particular dioceses. This power, within the confines of Canon Law and under the principle of the primacy of Rome, does not concern itself too much with official or referable matters, but centers about the person of the bishop and his actions within his own diocese. Depending on his inclinations, he can exercise an enormous influence over secular activities, ranging from social issues to ordinary entertainment, that will stamp his personal (and therefore private) impress on the actions of the Church and its people. He can prefer labor or he can mingle with radical right organizations, and no one can gainsay him this privilege. In this regard, imagine the feelings of a liberal whose bishop clearly aligns himself with, say, the John Birch Society. Without discussing the merits of either position, it is easy to see how so much that a bishop does can alienate the liberal.

The point is that though the bishops are our spiritual directors and thus are due obedience (something that scarcely evokes any reaction in the laity), they too often branch out into areas that are increasingly remote from their primary responsibility and even competence. But these areas of distinction are largely ignored, and whatever position a bishop takes in largely temporal affairs (granting the great difficulty often of distinguishing between what is within the realm of the "spiritual shepherd" and what is beyond his authority) is assumed to be a quasi-official position of the Church. This is true even in the many instances of bishops taking positions that are in direct opposition to the pronouncements of Rome.

The sad fact is that many bishops begin their reigns as spiritual directors and finish their reigns as political, social, economic, and intellectual tyrants. Naturally, laymen can ignore the politics and social doctrines of their bishop, but that isn't the point. When his personality plays so major a part in his tenure, it is bound to affect all those around him, down to the newest priest whose vow of obedience often covers matters beyond the purely spiritual, so that the whole diocese can be affected. The principle here is that coupling personality with power is dangerous. And power is a dangerous thing in itself, even when it is held in Christian hands.

It is a tremendous relief to pass on to the matters of papal influence and the papal office. By the grace of God, we have been granted an extraordinary succession of popes in the twentieth century, men whose personal ambitions have been conspicuous by their absence, men whose universal love, the apogee of which resided in the benign person of the late Pope John, has been felt by the great majority of non-Catholics as well as Catholics. These latter-day popes are in profound contrast with those who nearly brought the Church to its knees in the depths of the Renaissance and could well serve as prototypes of numerous modern bishops and priests.

I hope I have made it clear that the laity's discontent

stems from temporal transgressions, not spiritual. This discontent, threatening as it does to break out in anticlericalism, should actually be received by the clergy as a sign of concern for the Church. And I must pause to make an observation that may surprise a number of clerics, particularly those who have never known anything but the congenital comforts of Catholicism. There is a school of thought that, once a Catholic, always a Catholic. While this may be theologically well founded, it doesn't mean that a layman can't simply walk out of the Church for the last time; nor does it mean that a layman has to do any more than passively allow the sacraments to pass through his life. A layman always has options.

What is significant is that so many laymen care so much for the Church that they are willing to overcome the tradition of centuries of silence and raise their voices in protest. It would be erroneous to read into this a peasant revolt or some new sort of "modernism." A truly dissatisfied layman in revolt against both clergy and Church would not protest. He would simply get out of the Church (as many thousands do each year). He would not remain to take issue with the abuses he sees and wants to do away with, *not* because they merely offend him but more significantly because they offend the Church, which is far greater and far more important than the corporate structure currently being examined.

Inherent in the present discussion is the matter of the function of the layman in the Church. This complex question will not be settled in a single season of effort or thought. Indeed, for almost two thousand years we have lived with the question and have not evolved anything like a definitive answer. Despite this, we can explore several aspects of the problem.

To begin with, the nature and functions of the layman reside in a mystery not unlike that surrounding the hypostatic union, the perplexing fact of Christ's being both man and God. The layman resides both in the City of God and in the City of Man. He has a foot in each, and we can never make up our minds where one city leaves off and the other begins. In contrast to the cleric, who, while in this world, is not of it, the layman actually is partially not of this world though he *is* of this world. While we could concentrate almost endlessly on this riddle and probably never solve it, we would do better to look into the matter of what the layman is *not*.

The layman is not a pair of hands at someone else's disposal. It was once possible for the local pastor or bishop to rely on personal wisdom to solve the problems of his parish or diocese, but those were the simple days when farming was the rule and boys and girls were content to subsist on the intellectual pablum of the three R's. Or in an urban setting, the laymen were immigrants who needed lessons in the language far more than the spiritual consolations available at the nearest rectory.

What has been missing in the Church has been the layman's *mind*. The layman may supply hands, but scarcely ever has he been invited to offer his mind. In any instance, in any situation, it is the mind of the corporate structure that sets the course. The result is that the layman's mind is reactive rather than active in the Church's life. This is a disservice rendered by the corporate structure to the entire Mystical Body. It is as if less than one percent of the Mystical Body has intelligence while over ninety-nine percent can be only a reactive agent. This is obviously nonsense. The temptation is present to set forth all the things the layman can do, but that must come later. The point here is that the laity can be of active service only when the clergy, deep in their corporate structure, change their *attitude*.

This is a most significant fact that must not be ignored. The clergy call for lay participation. But if they presume that the laity will be content merely to serve as hands, the clergy are in for a terrible disappointment. The laity simply won't have that sort of thing any more. If the clergy lodge their request for lay help in traditional terms, I'm afraid the laity won't hear the call. To put it in vulgar terms, we've had it. We are simply finished with a system that clearly marks us as second-class Catholics, that allows us to serve, serve, serve, *ad nauseam.*

I have extended the discussion of traditional clerical attitudes because I feel that they constitute the most serious obstacle to major change within the Church, change currently being formulated by Vatican II. While it is quite clear that emphasis is being shifted to contending ideologies within the Church and that the long lay-clerical dichotomy is being bridged in the process, nevertheless this realignment is both very new and not appreciated by very many people. Basically we still divide the Church into those who think, act, and direct and those who merely follow in silent obedience.

When we view the alignment of the minority "conservatives" and the majority "liberals" in Vatican II, we see a clear expression of the Church's intent; but when we view the traditional alignment throughout the Catholic community, we see a vastly different situation. If "liberalism" marks the Council, then definitely "conservatism" marks everything else. It is quite true that what I have described as the percolation principle serves to dissipate any intent, but far more serious is the inertia that probably best characterizes human institutions. And it is this inertia, as personified by the great mass of the clergy, that endangers the efforts of Vatican II.

Before proceeding, however, I must point out that I am not implying that the clergy alone suffer from inertia; the laity are equally at fault. But it is the clergy and only the clergy who possess the authority and the power to effect changes within the Church. Even a gifted layman, like Jacques Maritain, can do a little more than present a thesis; the active participation of the corporate structure is required before it can be implemented. The difference is between a plan and a program.

Today the two most recurring pleas are for more priests and greater participation by the laity. A third should be made: reform the seminary system.

Again, to illustrate quickly the subject of seminary training, let me insert a personal experience. For a long time, we who are associated with *Ramparts* have been deeply concerned with all aspects of Catholic education, and in one area of the problem we were able to organize a serious study. However, when we considered (at the request of several clerical friends) the subject of seminary education, we ran into an almost insoluble difficulty. In private conversation as well as in correspondence, nearly universal discontent with seminary training was expressed on all sides. And yet, when we tried to settle on possible writers, we were hopelessly balked. Obviously, no layman could write since he would have no true knowledge of the situation. We thought of several articulate seminarians from various parts of the country, young men we knew to be extremely percipient, but we had to discard them since their act of criticism would seriously jeopardize their careers. The same difficulty presented itself when we considered a number of priests; they could scarcely get their criticisms past Church censors, or if somehow they did their careers would also be jeopardized. There remained only two possibilities, ex-seminarians or ex-priests, both of which we rejected because of the obvious *ad hominem* attacks that would be launched against them.

The consequence of all this has been that we find it impossible to explore the subject of seminary education. This impossibility reveals the serious flaw in Catholic thinking: that one outside the corporate structure may not criticize what goes on within, and that one within the structure cannot criticize anything without prior permission from a higher authority. This, of course, absolutely trammels the concept of free speech. It is difficult enough for the layman to try to explore certain areas, but his lot is far easier than that of the cleric who can't say or write anything without first clearing it upstairs. We laymen may have a bishop disown what we say, but at least we can speak. The poor priest is silenced by a higher authority which thrives on the vow of obedience, a most censorious power when in the wrong hands and when used for improper purposes. But this is the sort of thing we have, and it stifles serious inquiry into practices that have grown up within the Church. This particular practice of censorship is precisely what prevents entry into all other fields of investigation.

But more than censorship is involved; we also face the threat of complacency, the attitude that prefers the familiar to the experimental and the unknown. Worst of all is habit. Our Church has been functioning this way for centuries, and we have grown very used to it. Besides, we don't really know anything else except traditional clerical primacy, lay passivity, hierarchical supremacy, and our regular seminary system. We have always had prior censorship of clerical speech, we have always addressed the bishop as "excellency" and genuflected and kissed the episcopal ring, Latin is so much a part of our Catholic way of life, and Rome has always had its special and exclusive primacy. It is this habitual way of looking at things that will prove the greatest obstacle to fulfilling the promises of Vatican II.

Probably the most difficult habit we will have to overcome is that which characterizes most disastrously the system of seminary education. To begin with, a change must be made in the common posture of militant defense of the faith. Combative apologetics must give way to serious inquiry into realities, in matters both within the Church and outside. The curriculum must include more than carefully chosen segments of independent disciplines that lend themselves to quick memorization but fail to challenge anything other than bare memory. No soul was ever saved by a convenient syllogism.

Indeed, the greatest error is to rest Christianity on intellectualism, particularly when this intellectualism is not free and when it stresses logic rather than charity. The most seriously neglected area of seminary inquiry is that which is instinctual, that which is barely sensed by the intellect but is fully experienced by the heart. This involves the arts, such as literature, music, and painting, as well as psychology, sociology, and all the other disciplines that concern the human personality, which are currently neglected stepchildren in seminary education. Here is the prime fault in the system as it now stands. The system proclaims that the mind, if sufficiently fed, can provide the spiritual manna man needs. It fails to feed the heart, and it is the heart that feeds the soul.

An example of this disorientation can be found in a most unfortunate article that appeared in *America* several years ago. It purported to deal with the subject of fall-out shelter morality. The article made it syllogistically clear that if a shelter owner were driven to extremities, he could kill a neighbor who tried to gain entry into the shelter. The clerical mind that formulated the principle did a remarkable job of pleading the case. In fact, it was so logical, so perfectly reasoned, that one felt almost tempted to buy a gun. Almost—but not quite. The fatal flaw in the argument lay in the fact that it was just that: an argument which could appeal to the mind and even obtain intellectual assent, but which utterly failed to appeal to the human heart. It was telling the mind to shoot, while it told the heart that it would be the victim of that final shot from the mind. No Christian could possibly accept such a deadly solution.

Some time later, in the same magazine (this is not intended to be a criticism of *America;* it is just coincidence), a clerical author wrote an article setting forth the reasons that special protection should be given to priests in the event of an atomic attack. It was pointed out that priests would be needed more than ever since so many people would be dying and would therefore require the last sacraments. Again, the argument satisfied the mind; it made sense; but it also horrified the conscience. If it were valid, then priests would have to make the necessary plans; but they would also have to remain silent about them lest they scandalize all Christendom. Of course, the argument is totally false. It fails to take into account the promises of Christ that the Church will endure till the end of time. And it exposes the most fundamental fallacy of all in clerical attitudes.

Basically, what we have is the formal principle that Christ made certain promises, among them that we have the continuing presence of the Holy Ghost to guarantee continual holiness till the end of time. In reality, what we have is a Church in which the corporate structure presumes that it and it alone can speak for the Church—not only that, but speak quite infallibly on matters far beyond the strict limits of faith and morals. The converse of this is also presumed: that those outside the structure are simply incapable of distinguishing between Catholic truth and common error.

This remarkable state of affairs arises out of a misconception about the nature of the Church. When our Lord said, ". . . thou art Peter, and upon this rock I shall build my Church, and the gates of hell shall not prevail against *it"* (italics mine), He was very explicit; the Church shall not be prevailed against. Further, our Lord was again very explicit when He said that the Holy Ghost would preserve and guard the *Church* to the end of time, not just a *segment* of it. Therefore, when a member of the corporate structure speaks or acts, when a layman speaks or acts, each and all, in any particular instance, can be either right or wrong; but still we have Christ's promise that between now and eternity the Church will remain holy.

This involves the actions of the Holy Ghost far more than those of the priest or the layman. *Despite* us, one could say, the Church will remain holy. Too much dependence on ourselves and not enough on the Holy Ghost have brought the Church perilously close to ruin at various times in its history, but by Christ's promise the Church has endured and always will. This is not to preach presumption; God acts through His instrumentalities as a general rule, and upon their prudence, wisdom, and love much of the Church's life is dependent. But if we falter, much to our discredit, the Holy Ghost is always there to preserve the Church. And when I speak of the Church, I mean the Mystical Body of Christ, which includes within its confines not only the clergy but the laity as well.

As I said at the beginning of this chapter, a revolution is taking place, and the Church is centrally involved. It is from this revolution, as it unfolds itself in the next few years, that we will find a new Church emerging. Unhappily, every birth has its pangs, and what we now bring forth will be born in pain; but the pain, like Good Friday, must be endured so that we may come to the blessed day of Easter.

Part of this pain will arise from a realignment of traditional forces, and part from a severance from much of the past that has so hurt the Church. Probably the greatest new force in the revolution will be the laity, who even now are tendering their most potent gift: the gift of their minds, revealing themselves not in controversy but in contribution.

2

THE NEGRO QUESTION: WHY?

IT is fashionable to state that America is in a great moral crisis because of the presence of the Negro. We all tend to consider the aspirations of the Negro as being legitimately his to realize as a citizen, and we generally agree in theory that the only deceent thing to do is grant him equal citizenship. After all, we are the noble experiment in democracy, and we boast of the Declaration of Independence and the Constitution, particularly the Thirteenth and Fourteenth Amendments, which so forthrightly proclaim public principles of justice and equality. We allow Negroes to demonstrate in the streets, Northern streets, and we of the North shake our heads disapprovingly when Southern police play hoses on Negro children before hauling them off to jail. We listen, with varying degrees of attention, to men like Roy Wilkins, Martin Luther King, and James Baldwin, and agree that something should be done—theoretically. Or if we transcend theory, we urge some sort of action, generally elsewhere.

However, what is popularly stated is not necessarily the truth. We are not yet in a crisis; and contrary to another popular assertion we are not yet in a revolution—at least, the white man isn't.

After generations of deafness, we have finally heard the Negro voice raised in protest. We accept the fact of this protest. But we don't really appreciate the challenge that accompanies the Negro protest. The Negro is telling us of the white community that he is not going to accept second-class citizenship and that he is determined to be a full member of American society. While we hear his words, we don't fully believe them. We still expect that displays of violence and repression in the South, combined with protracted committee meetings in the North, will dent his ambitions so effectively that he will start tipping his hat once more and saying, "Yassah, boss," all the while exposing his teeth in a servile and anxious grin. But we are wrong. The Negro will not back down; he will perish first. The revolution, the real crisis, will come for the white man when he actually realizes that the Negro means what he says. *Then* we will have to prepare our final answer to his demands.

The difficulty in approaching the whole subject rests on the white man's inability to see the Negro for what he is. But more is wrong: the white man is equally unable to appreciate what has brought the Negro to his present situation.

One of the great misconceptions held by the white man is that the Negro is primarily seeking school integration, job opportunities, desegregated bathroom facilities and lunch counters, voting rights, and the off chance of mingling socially with whites. To talk of these things is merely to dwell on indicia. What the Negro wants is a sense of identity, a sense of his own inherent significance as a man.

Several centuries ago the Negro was wrenched out of his own culture and auctioned into another. He had no choice. As chattel, he endured the equivocal status of being both an animal and personal property. He worked and bred. But he couldn't live in a vacuum; he needed some cultural context. Lacking his former milieu, he had to relate to something, so he took the only one available—the white man's culture. What developed, particularly following emancipation, was a caricature, a distortion of the real thing. No Negro could really emulate whites, for the simple reason that he was not white. He was a Negro and, as a minor segment, was subject to the majority. He could not rise above a carefully prescribed level; he could not challenge the white man. It was essential that the Negro realize the cardinal fact of his existence: he was inferior. The white man determined that.

Now, having no past to return to and having no future to strive for, where could the Negro turn in order to find an identity? He was not an African, and yet he was not an American. He floated in a social limbo. Of course, the white man saw none of this. He believed that the Negro was happy, or possibly he wished to believe that the Negro was happy. But he never saw into the Negro's heart.

Adding to the illusion of contentment was the principle of accommodation graciously described by Booker T.

Washington in a speech; he likened the races to the fingers of a man's hand—separate, but equal. The principle of accommodation, it must be pointed out, was actually an alternative to something worse. In this temporary surrender, the Negro was at least given a chance to endure through one of the worst and most dangerous periods of his existence. Washington and other Negroes spoke through weakness; strength lay with the white man, who over the years constructed (in the South visibly and in the North invisibly) the barbaric hypocrisy of separate but equal institutions.

The moral significance of this social anomaly lies in the fact that it was impressed on the Negro by the white and was maintained by force. The Negro could only accept the situation in silence; the white man saw to that. Needless to say, this did not serve to establish his identity or his dignity, except on the white man's terms. The dominant rationale for this treatment was that the Negro was inferior. Not only was his intellect low, but he was a slave to lust, lazy, deceitful, unreliable; and most telling of all, it was ordained by God that he be inferior to the white man. God had spoken and the nigger better listen!

Listen he did—for generations—but locked out of the white man's sight were the visions that some day would be transformed into reality; beyond the white man's hearing were the whispered aspirations that would some day become the roar of black emancipation. The Negro has climbed the mountain, and the white man can do nothing to stop him because the world has changed.

As of now, the white man protests; history works for

him, and yet paradoxically the emerging world works against him. The singular error committed by most of us, Northerners and Southerners, black and white, is that of misreading the times. Today doesn't exist isolated from the past; neither does tomorrow contain a truth not promised today. The American white man (particularly but not peculiarly in the South) must reckon with the past and prepare for the future. The white man, so much a victim as well as provoker of his ways, lives in the social and moral vortex that he has largely created but can't rid himself of. He stoked the furnace of tragedy but now can't quite bring himself to damp the fire—and this, out of fear.

With a history of authoritarian domination, the white man has found it virtually impossible to let the reins loose, largely out of fear of retribution. His conscience, burdened so terribly with guilt over his infamous crime of enslaving, cannot imagine a modern emancipation without retribution. Who can confess to centuries of oppression without anticipating reprisal, a hatred to match his own, a divine accounting for so much evil? Only a conversion to sanctity with its simple acceptance of penance could assure the guilty of a *charitable* reaction—not revenge but compassion, as one side of mutual compassion. For every one crucified there is a crucifier, and who deserves the greater compassion? The solution to this pitiful state in American society lies in the crucified segment's granting forgiveness. *This will be,* because of the Negro's almost infinite capacity to love (could anything else explain his extraordinary history?) and the white man's conscience.

The end is not yet in sight; indeed, we are only at the

beginning of the ultimate travail. We will go through the
fire of fear, hatred (or rather self-hatred), violence, deception, protestations, until we reach ultimate purification.
But—and this is the heart of the matter—we must go
through this American Good Friday to reach peace. Only
when the Negro establishes his identity will the white man
establish *his* true identity. Only when membership in American society is equally shared by Negroes and whites will
there be a national identity.

Crucial in this mutuality of membership is the awareness and the calm acceptance of difference. No imagination
is so mad as to conclude that the Negro is indistinguishable
from the white man. Primarily the difference is a matter of
color, and we must be able to stare this color down. This is
not to say we should all become color-blind, but rather that
we should be aware of this shallow difference as we are aware
of the difference in the colors of eyes, in the span of a man's
reach. Color and breadth are merely accidental to the substance, which is man's relationship with God. Does God
love the Negro less? Or more? Either in inconceivable.

Therein lies the ultimate test of all relationships—their
merit with God. Beyond this there is nothing worth men-
tioning.

While God's love is real and evident, man's isn't. It is no
secret that most white men don't like the Negro as a person.
As an object worthy of some sort of status in a "democratic" system, he is tolerated more or less as an abstract
principle, but as a *person* he is unloved.

There is a particular poignancy to the present situation
in America. The Negro, straining so vigorously for recogni-

tion, uses every method imaginable—demonstrations in the South, sit-ins, picketing Northern building sites, organizing committees to confer with white counterparts, lawsuits to open previously all-white schools, and so on. The white reaction to all this, at least among "liberals," was at first to applaud it as the right sort of thing to do; but lately whites have begun to protest against the principle of "compensation" for past injustices, according to which *more* is to be attempted for the Negro than for the white. Along with their more conservative kin, the "liberals" claim that whites will be discriminated against. They miss the point; we *owe* the Negro a great deal and we must redeem our moral debt.

Yes, we must overcompensate, not merely to help the Negro but also to allow us to do this penance so that the moral imbalance can be righted at long last. We must increase our efforts toward conciliation with our Negro brethren who have been victims of our immoral conduct. But this "compensation" cannot be meted out solely in the form of jobs and education. What is needed more than anything else is the total integration of hearts. And this we have not done, are not doing, and I fear probably will not do.

The problem of the Negro in America is not his problem; it is the white man's. We created the Negro plight and now the Negro is holding himself up as a mirror to us. The Negro is saying, "This is what you have done to your fellow man. This is the truth about yourselves, you who claim Christ for your Master. Now, what are you going to do? Are you going to admit the truth about yourselves, continue your immoral ways, and still claim Christ for your Master?

Or are you going to become the Christians you claim to be?"

This challenge is directed not only to all America but specifically toward the Catholic Church, which makes so many assertions about brotherly love. And we all know how the Church has reacted in the past and how it is reacting today. What is of greatest concern is whether the Church will ever exert the spiritual energy necessary to reverse its present role of followship to one of leadership in this moment of moral decision.

The Church (and here I am referring to all Catholics, lay and clerical) has acted shamefully in the racial situation that has plagued this nation. We Catholics love to pretend that we are not biased against any man because of race since we are all brothers in Christ. But we know better because we have the facts.

We have the fact of papal encyclicals that proscribe racism in unequivocal terms, but we also have the fact of racism within the Church in the South. While some brave bishops have broken down inherited barriers, there are others who not only refuse to accept papal encyclicals but actively foster racism, though with token lip service to Rome. They incite prejudice by cleverly worded pastoral letters which reassure their white Catholics that there is no timetable for integration of the school system; that the Negro, though our brother in Christ, must earn the right to equality; that "special circumstances" allow for local violation of the fundamental tenet of Catholic faith that all men are equal before God. These escape clauses cannot go unchallenged.

What best identifies the principle of "special circumstances" is expediency. The theory is that though Church social doctrine says one thing, a local bishop can avoid applying the social doctrine by claiming special circumstances; that is, "special circumstances" can be cited as militating against Christian morality and therefore immorality will be allowed to flourish in its place. In other words, we will tolerate an evil in order to keep the sacraments going to those very people whose social conscience in any other geographic area and under another bishop would deny them access to any sacrament except penance. In the Catholic Church racism is a grave sin, and no protestations of special circumstances or mask of prudence can alter that one basic fact, the opinions of various Southern bishops to the contrary notwithstanding.

It is interesting to note how firm and forthright some bishops are when they take their stand on abortion, birth control, and divorce (the ABCD's of modern Catholicism) and how they equivocate when grave social issues invade their chanceries. The reason for this inconsistency can be suggested: as to the A's, B's, C's, and D's the bishops are not personally involved in any way. However, when a community is afflicted with a social disease for which the most universal social principles of the Church clearly indicate the course the local bishop should take, we have the odd circumstance of the bishop's being personally involved. The Catholic community will take issue with him and if necessary will apply the severest countermeasure available— economic withdrawal. The powerful laymen are those with the most money to lavish on the Church, and not surprisingly they are the very ones with the most conservative social views and the greatest vested interests to preserve against any social or economic change.

While we may criticize various local bishops, there is a more significant criticism that should be leveled against laymen who exert unconscionable pressure. And yet here we face the ultimate choice of faith, and here, when grave issues are at stake, we must assert our true Christianity by resisting evil pressures for the sake of social justice. The way of the prophets was not easy, the death of the martyrs was not a gentle one; and a Christlike position will not be easily maintained by our modern bishops (or anyone else who claims to be Christian) in the face of the vile attitude of the many lay people who practice the sin of racial prejudice while insisting on the sacraments.

So pervasive is this evil that in various Southern communities a Negro Catholic cannot receive our Lord in communion until all the whites have had their go at the rail *and* until they have returned to their segregated seats in the Church. There are "colored" parishes and "white" parishes in sections of the South. Indeed, so extensive is this sacrilege that in certain areas, if a Negro legitimately misses mass in his "colored" church, he is relieved of the obligation to attend mass that Sunday rather than be required to attend a "white" church. And beyond all this, Negro priests in these areas are just as segregated as their lay brethren. *Christ segregated!*

We are all guilty. We do not need to point a moral finger at the South; we have horrors enough in the North to gag even the most indelicate conscience. The only difference between the Northern Church and the Southern Church (so we are divided) is that we of the North are more subtle, more covert, in our sins. We don't have segregated churches, although there is the courteous evasion based on *de facto* geographic segregation. We allow Negroes in our churches and even let them (here we practice consummate charity) receive our Lord right next to us. Of course, there are so few in our better parishes that they are more curiosities than afflictions. But in those other parishes where they are *not* curiosities, we give them pew space only reluctantly, as if just barely obeying the injunction to love one's neighbor by tolerating his presence, without accepting his person.

In 1963 the American bishops issued a joint pastoral letter that eloquently denounced racism. In terms reminiscent of gentle John XXIII, the letter called for Christian brotherhood and leveled the severest censures against any person or group practicing the sin of racism. And yet, because of "special circumstances" the pastoral letter of the American bishops was not read in portions of the South.

The solution will not be found in pastoral letters. The way is not to denounce various bishops who merely personify our secret prejudices. What is needed is our personal and individual conversion to Christianity.

The North, the East, the West should feel no vain conceit in this matter. We have the open fact of discrimination within the Northern Church. Although the American bishops have issued their pastoral letter, although various dioceses have organized Catholic interracial councils, although numbers of laymen and clergy have begun, though belatedly, to seek an end to this evil, there still remains the interior mood of the vast majority of Catholics, who look down on the Negro as something less. We give evidence of this by our refusal to do more than admit Negroes to the church building and to the sacraments found inside. Let us rather talk in terms of the various church groups, such as the sodalities and the Knights of Columbus. Let us talk about the presence of Negroes in our homes. It is when the Negro seeks entry into our personal lives that we turn away. He can come into the Church proper, but he is unwelcome in the Church improper.

And yet we seek converts. If I were a Negro, I would laugh at the Catholic Church for its obvious hypocrisy, just as I would laugh in all white faces. But I am not a Negro, and in silence I have to stand by and watch him love what he should despise. Somewhere in all this is a sublime mystery.

White supremacists, in all their cleverness, raise the chimera of mongrelization when they pose what is intended to be the final question on race: "Would you want your daughter to marry one?" This is truly a remarkable revelation of the state of mind in which virtually all of us live, because the instinctive answer, accompanied by a deep shudder of revulsion, should be a hateful "No!" Oddly enough, the question is a fair one, and our individual answer will honestly expose our true feelings far more than a formal assent to the American bishops' pastoral letter.

I don't think it is unfair to assume that the question of racial intermarriage is intended to conjure up pictures of one's pale and innocent daughter being linked to an ignorant, bestial, sex-mad black man, exuding some repulsive

smell peculiar to the Negro race, whose eyes roll as he las-
civiously drools while raping the young lady in some sexual
frenzy far beyond white imagination (or is this a secret
sexual ambition of the white Puritan?). If he sticks to one's
daughter, something *they* rarely do, the black beast will
beat her, assault her, and in the end get himself thrown in
jail or executed for raping any white woman he can put his
hands on.

The fact is that if we are going to discuss the matter of
interracial marriage, we must do so in the same terms with
which we approach all other discussions of marriage,
namely, in terms of love. In opposition to the specter raised
by white supremacists, I would suggest the following
choices.

In the first place, let us suppose the same pale and innocent daughter married to a white moral and sexual degenerate who not only subjects her to physical abuse and habitual abandonment but also forces her into the same sexual
depravity one attributes to the above Negro. Further, to
maintain the prejudiced parallel, there is no assertion of
love.

In contrast to this, let us assume a young man and a
young woman who follow the usual social patterns of association that may eventually lead to marriage. Suppose, as
so often happens, that they meet in college or at work and
that they discover first friendship and then love. They live in
more or less comparable circumstances, and the young man
is preparing for or already engaged in some profession such
as law. And finally, assume (as we do for the ordinary
marriage) that they love one another. The only thing out of

the ordinary is that the man is a Negro and the girl is your daughter. Which would you prefer, that she marry the degenerate white man or this Negro? The answer will reveal whether you are prejudiced against color, and further, whether you think love can exist between a Negro and a white.

There is another dimension to this matter of race. If the white girl, or for that matter a white man, married someone of the Negro race (again, on the basis of love), the white partner would have the awesome opportunity of sharing the pain the Negro experiences. It is easy to share the pain of one's ordinary spouse in ordinary circumstances, but how much more sharpened is the demand for love when it nests in the perpetual pain of one's beloved! *This* is true love.

But love doesn't live an isolated existence. An unavoidable consequence of interracial marriage is pain, pain for one's spouse and pain over the abuse and torment experienced by the children of this union. The tragedy is that the loved ones are not at fault; it is society that provides the pain and abuse that is at fault. The innocent lovers are the victims.

And how do we Catholics fit into this modern tragedy? We are part of that society which would punish those who love in opposition to our demand that they hate one another. We of the Church profess a primary loyalty to our faith, and yet when it comes to displaying this faith in its social setting, we quickly abandon whatever we appear to believe in and take up the cudgels of racism. It is our shame that if we have a choice between the marriage of a white Catholic and a Negro Catholic or of a white Catholic and a white non-Catholic, we will choose the latter almost without exception. While we preach love and embrace the faith, we will embrace a white Christ only, not a black Christ. In the final analysis we are more race-oriented than we are religion-oriented. We deceive only ourselves; God and the Negro know better. And yet we receive the sacraments. How can we when we commit the grave sin of refusing to love our neighbor? We can't, but we do. And may God have mercy on our souls.

Finally, there is something that should haunt the soul of every white man as he gazes from so far away on the face of the Negro. It concerns the moment that enters every Negro's life when, as a child, he looks deeply into his mother's eyes and asks the eternal question, "Why?"

3 ✵

THE FINAL EQUATION

THERE is a disconcerting similarity between the situation of the American Negro in his efforts to establish a viable relationship with the American white and the situation of the Catholic layman in his efforts to establish a viable relationship with the Catholic clergy.

But before we proceed, it must be made abundantly clear that the present discussion is concerned neither with the causes that have produced the relational difficulties nor with any desire of the Negro or the layman to become what he is not—respectively, a white man or a priest. What we are concerned with here is viability, notwithstanding distinctions of race and classifications of Church members. Essentially we have a situation where the Negro *qua* Negro seeks to reconcile his relational difficulties with the white, and where the Catholic layman *qua* layman seeks to resolve his relational difficulties with the clergy. Neither problem is imagined; they are very real.

Whites often seem to assume Negroes wish to drain

away their color so that they can "pass over" and become white. This is simply not true, even in the face of the fact that many Negroes would appear to wish for some "passing over." But they are not seeking to become white in the affirmative sense; they are only trying to avoid the stigma of being palpably Negro, and their various efforts to become more like whites are negative.

On the bottom of Negro society is the thoroughly black, unadulterated Negro. This man is as far from being white as is genetically possible. And he is the least likely to be accepted by even the most "liberal" whites. In between this base creature and the exalted white, there are various gradations of color. In the hierarchy of things, the less the color, the straighter the hair, and the more distinctively white the features, such as thin lips and an aquiline nose, the higher is one's standing in Negro society. It is obvious that the Negro is race-conscious. However, this is not his doing. White society has brought this about. If color is the bar to acceptance by the white, it naturally follows that the lighter one is the more acceptable one is, and vice versa.

This acceptability, of course, has nothing to do with white society, which doesn't care how light a Negro's skin is. As the state of Virginia puts it, "so much as one drop" of Negro blood makes one a Negro, and so holds the rest of white America. The acceptability I am speaking of is within the Negro community itself. The basic rationale for this hierarchy is the avoidance of pain, a rationale introduced into Negro society by the white man.

Most white thinking errs by considering the Negro simplistically; he is either all beast or else he is just slightly less than the angles, depending on whether one is a white supremacist or a white "liberal." Every Negro, like every white, is actually somewhere in between, of course. He is the product of normal reproduction practices; he grows up, marries, procreates, and in time dies. He is husband, father, brother, and all the other relationships experienced by whites. He is capable of love, hate, jealousy, and other personality traits exhibited by whites. He is known to kill and be killed, whether in an alley or on a battlefield. He steals; and he is stolen from, particularly where his women are concerned. He prays and he curses. In short, he is a human being, and being thoroughly human he is subject to such human pressures as social and economic exploitation, political exclusion, and emotional tyranny, which have the same effect on him as they would on any other member of the human family.

The American Negro is a man who has largely been so distorted by white brutality, ranging from physical abuse to mental oppression, that it is exceedingly difficult to see him as he is, a human being, and as he could be if he had never suffered his particular history in America, a full-fledged member of American society. This peculiar status of the Negro in America is unique; nowhere else in the world is the black man (he is only a "Negro" in this country) in precisely the same condition of being half-slave, half-free. Even in the Union of South Africa he has a confirmed status (though despicable) and a cultural milieu of his own. In America he has neither. As has been said earlier, he is in his own limbo, awaiting deliverance.

This deliverance can come in part from the Negro's

own efforts, which efforts have been under way for a long time. I don't mean education and the development of skills, which scarcely qualify as minimal standards for entry into general society. I mean those forceful efforts that attack the conscience of the white man, such as demonstrations and legal actions. (Probably the saddest commentary on our white society is the fact that the vast majority of whites take the Negroes' efforts seriously only when white economic life is jeopardized.)

But the major effort at Negro deliverance will have to be made by the white segment of society. In their firm determination never to return to the past, Negroes face two alternatives. They will have to be destroyed (or put into "retirement camps," as Thomas Merton recently wrote), which will require the active cooperation of whites; or they can be equal members of American society, which will also require the active cooperation of whites.

In the latter case, both the Negro and the white will finally turn away from traditional patterns of thought and conduct, and each will share coextensively in the life of America. Whites and Negroes will compete socially, politically, economically, and intellectually on the basis of ability rather than color. What this will do is provide us with the opportunity to identify Negroes as individuals possessing or lacking this or that characteristic or capability. What it will bring to an end is the habit of labeling each Negro as a Negro instead of seeing him as a man whose role in society will depend on *him* and not on our own bigotry.

Once a full participant in American society, the Negro will remain a Negro and the white will remain a white.

Between them they will comprise society. This will be a different society from any we have ever had in this country, for missing will be oppression and present will be equality. From this will flow the full realization of our national potential, not in terms of things but in terms of morality. The pledge made at our national beginnings will be fulfilled in all its glory, that all men are created equal and endowed with certain inalienable rights.

Before proceeding with the analogy between the Negro and the Catholic layman, a further point must be made about equality. According to American morality, which includes American law, all men are equal. That is, in the eyes of the state and in the eyes of the law all men as men are indistinguishable. And yet, vis-à-vis each other, all men are not created equal. Each of us has his individual capabilities and incapacities. The athlete is not the scholar and the child is not the philosopher. Out of *this* inequality arises a hierarchy of order and authority within a given field of activity, such as exists within a business, a political structure, and so on. The key is competence, not color or race. It is not unlike the matter of vocation.

The Negro and the layman: what ultimately binds them in this discussion? The fact that each is part of something greater, but because of factors beyond his control, he is unable either to achieve his legitimate aspirations or to accept his equivocal status. To a large extent, what has been said of the Negro can be said of the Catholic layman.

The layman views his position in three ways: in terms of his relationship with the corporate structure, in terms of his relationship with the total Church (the entire Mystical

Body), and in terms of his relationship with himself. The Negro has his three considerations: toward the body of white society, toward the totality of American society, and toward himself. Just as the Negro has a sense of frustration toward white society, of personal inferiority, and of exclusion from the totality of American society, so does the layman have his sense of frustration toward the corporate structure, of personal inferiority, and finally of exclusion from full participation in the Catholic Church.

I might possibly disclose the feelings of both Negroes and laymen by distinguishing between common modes of expression and what both Negro and layman really want to be called. The common terms, which represent the attitudes that both Negro and layman are fighting against, are "the American Negro" and "the Catholic layman." While these two time-honored phrases are apparently innocuous, they expose a fundamental abuse. The fact is that in one the modifier *American* is used to describe a type of Negro, while in the other the modifier *Catholic* describes a type of layman. The point is that both *Negro* and *layman* are external to the modifier. What the Negro wants is to be termed "a Negro American," that is, an American who happens to be a Negro and not a Negro who happens to be an American. Similarly, the layman wants to be termed "a lay Catholic," that is, a Catholic who happens to be a layman and not a layman who happens to be a Catholic. Put differently, being a Negro or a layman should be incidental to being American or Catholic, not the reverse, which tends to place each somewhat outside of that society with which he seeks identification. Indeed, only if the common concepts are reversed can either establish an authentic sense of identity. As it is, the Negro never feels quite like an American and the layman never feels quite like a Catholic.

The reason for both should be obvious. Though by circumstance each is actually an integral member of his particular society, the dominant entity of that society says, directly or indirectly, that such is not the case. Neither does this in the obvious way of denying membership. In fact, quite the opposite is true: each particular society insists that the Negro or layman is a true member. However, the principle of equality is missing. And equality rests solidly on the principle of the dignity of each member of society, whether American or Catholic. You deprive a man of his dignity when you deprive him of his potency, that is, his capacity to act. Conversely, you make him impotent by only allowing him the function of reacting to the activity of another. And it is here that we find the bond common to the Negro American and the lay Catholic.

The white American and the clerical Catholic have assumed positions that are not legitimately theirs; neither transcends his own society; each is a segment of something greater. What they have assumed is this: the white American believes that he completely and exclusively fills American society; the clergy implies that in its corporate structure it is somehow independent of the general Catholic society.

It is the first unwarranted assumption that has forced American society into its present travail, and it is the second that forced the Catholic Church into its present Vatican Council. It is not difficult to see in Birmingham a mirror of the Catholic struggle in Rome. While the jailing of Negroes may seem terribly different from the formal and modulated actions in St. Peter's Basilica, there is the historic fact that both are strenuous efforts by the two societies to resolve the complex question of their identity. Birmingham asks the question: what is American society? The Vatican Council asks the question: what is the Catholic Church? Both have been a long time coming. Each reveals the interesting fact that neither the Church nor American society is content, that each feels something is drastically wrong, that somewhere in time what once was can no longer be. In both there are the two great extremes of ancient conservatism and modern liberalism, so that the ultimate conflict in both is occurring between those who want nothing changed and those who press for change.

Call it reform? Better to call it a reshaping. Because what will come out of all this is a reshaping of the very segments that have produced the travail confronted, a reshaping arising out of the impotency of both the Negro and the layman, neither of whom brought the travail about. Only those with the power to act can act; yet there is a growing *sense* of potency on the part of the Negro and the layman, although this sense has yet to be translated into the *experience* of potency. The growing self-awareness of each is taking form not in terms of those who dominate them but in terms of themselves. Each has caught sight of his own inherent worth.

It is no sham when men like Martin Luther King speak in terms of Christian love and meet violence with Christian nonviolence. Two things make this possible: genuine love for those who have oppressed them and a corresponding self-love (not to be confused with conceit), which have their foundations in a love of God. The same thing is true of the layman, who loves God, himself, and quite naturally his clerical brethren.

Precisely because of this love does the Negro seek to end the moral bondage in which the white man finds himself. The white man is the Negro's brother. It is the white man who suffers from the guilt of oppression, and the Negro seeks to lift this burden from his white brother. The Negro is not guilty; the white man is.

It is no easy thing to take the next inescapable step in the comparison of the Negro and the layman, but the step must be taken if we are honestly to analyze the basis for much that disturbs the Church. In more than a cerebral sense the layman loves his clerical brethren who are comembers of the Mystical Body. Bound up in this love, however, is the tragic awareness that the clergy, in its attitude of superiority, has effected practices over the centuries which have placed the laity in a specifically inferior position. Laymen are directed to be passive, obedient, and silent. Authority rests solely with the clergy. Initiative rests with the clergy. Potency rests with the clergy.

The effect of this is to deny the layman full entry into the Church, and here I am still speaking of the totality of Catholic society, not the corporate structure. What the clergy has said in the past and is by and large still saying to the laity (and how this mirrors the painful situation of the Negro!) is, "You are Catholics, inescapably and forever, but you are not to engage yourselves except as we direct. It is a question not of your having rights by virtue of being Catholic, but of your functioning by virtue of what we decide. And in this decision we are right." This is to say that the laity cannot look to God's mandate, but only to that of the clergy.

The result of both white and clerical domination has been to prevent the full development of the Negro and the layman. The obvious retort to this allegation is to challenge both the Negro and the layman to state what this theoretical fulfillment is supposed to be. It is indeed a difficult challenge to meet, since neither the Negro nor the layman has any ideal to work toward; for centuries, each has had to assume such an unnatural posture that neither can imagine what it would be like to achieve an upright stance. Still, certain generalities will help.

The Negro says he wants to be fully American, that is, to vote, hold decent jobs, go to school, and so on. But since these are merely external evidence of something internal, they don't really answer the question. What then is this "something internal" that is so important? It is two things, or rather two internal states: that of the Negro and (in a sense more importantly) that of the white man. The Negro wishes to be a man, a man of dignity and of inherent worth—in short, man as created by God, man made in the image of God. He wishes to stand upright. But because of his tragic history, he lacks the psychological freedom necessary to do so. So long bent over, his ego must wait upon the liberation of the white man's own ego, which, when free, will thrust aside the past and recognize the Negro for what he is: a man no less and no more than he. Then and only then will the Negro ego be able to stand erect. The key to understanding is the fact that the Negro ego is bent, not by choice but by the the force the white man has exerted.

I have purposely discussed the situation of the Negro as a means of describing the lay situation by indirection. This was a method of preparing for something far closer to home and far more subject to dangerous emotional (rather than analytical) responses. Just as the white man is excessively sensitive to anything that challenges his most central being, his conscience, so too the clergy can be expected to react hypersensitively, particularly when so many clerics haven't had the slightest inkling of laymen's feelings and haven't imagined in all their lives that this Church of ours is anything less than a large and happy family.

What, then, of lay fulfillment in the Church? Following the points developed around the Negro's desire to be a member of American society, we can begin by stating that the layman seeks dignity, inherent worth as a Catholic. With great validity we can claim that the layman feels his ego has been bent by outside forces that are themselves bent, and we can plead that the outside ego correct itself and thus grant the layman the psychological freedom he needs to stand erect. But when all this is done, where are we?

I said a bit earlier that the nature and the function of the layman is a mystery. And here, the layman's case is distinguishable from that of the Negro. In the Negro's case we can point to sufficient externals, such as voting and educational equality, and sufficient internals that add up to totality of membership in American society. Can we do the same for the layman—that is, draw up a list of the suf-

ficient internal and external elements that would add up to
totality of membership in the Catholic Church? I don't think
so, because just as the layman is a mystery, so too is the
Church. This problem is made more complicated by the fact
that while it is within the nature of a Negro to be, say,
President of the country, no layman can be a priest, unless
he ceases to be a layman. While we can formulate a brief
legalism to describe a Catholic, whether lay or clerical, by
listing communion with Rome, baptism, and possession of
faith, we can do little more without the discussion becoming
constructional, that is, describing one Catholic who becomes a cleric and the other who *remains* a layman. Perhaps here we have the first opening to unraveling the mystery. When a layman (and all clerics were once laymen)
becomes a cleric, he becomes something *more* than Catholic. But can that be? Obviously not. Well, then, what does
he become? *This* is the riddle. *This* is the problem.

What a marvelous example of serendipity! All the
while we are searching out the mystery of the layman while
actually he poses no mystery at all. We all know what a layman is; he is a member of the Mystical Body of Christ (in
communion with Rome, baptized, and in possession of
faith). The layman, like *any* Catholic, is a witness for
Christ, and his mission is to serve as Christ's priest on earth
for the purpose of redeeming all mankind that they might
achieve life everlasting. The layman, like *any* Catholic, lives
in this world while preparing for the next. He is obligated to
do his best to live a sanctified life, in the process of which
he seeks not only to know God better but also to help others
know God better, not only to serve God better but also to

help others serve God better, not only to love God better but also help others love God better. This, then, is the layman, a very simple man to describe. There is no mystery to him at all. In his own society he is exactly analogous to the Negro, who can best be described—who can only be described one way—as an American. Any other characteristic is merely a detail, the least important of which is the fact that his skin is a certain color (even that isn't "certain" since his color can range from virtual white to the blackest black).

The real problem centers around the nature of the clergy, who have all the characteristics of the laity, who in turn are entire Catholics. (I hope by now no one will advance the nonsense that he is something less than an entire Catholic.) It is like an equation:

$$X \text{ (the layman)} = 21$$
$$Y \text{ (the clergy)} = 21$$
$$\therefore X = Y$$

And yet they are different, we are told, despite the immutable law which states that things equal to the same thing are equal to each other. How can this be explained? Here we have a layman and a cleric each of whom is an entire Catholic. This should lead to the statement that the layman equals the cleric, or that the layman *is* the cleric. And this we know to be nonsensical. If there is one thing we laymen know, it is that we are not equal to the clergy.

The only solution to the situation where logic says one thing and the senses say another is to conclude that the senses are wrong. And the quickest way to demonstrate the fallacy of the senses is to restate the equation as follows:

$$X \text{ (the layman)} = 21$$
$$Y \text{ (the clergy)} = XXI$$
$$\therefore X \neq Y$$

As you can see, the clergy uses Roman numerals, while the layman doesn't.

Unfortunately, we can't rest a very serious discussion on so facile a demonstration, although it is a quick formula easily remembered that does serve to dramatize the situation. Far more significant is the fact that in *essence* there is no difference between laity and clergy. What difference there is depends solely upon *form,* that is, the form that the Catholicism of each takes. The mystery, if there is any, is concerned with the human mystery of why men find it necessary to feel superior to their fellow men.

4 ❧

THE MIRROR
OF DISCONTENT

"I AM a Catholic."

At first blush this brief admission (or representation) seems to be a rather precise, even summary, statement of a particular man's nature. If we were to peer more closely at the concept "I am a Catholic," we would quite naturally come to the formal elaboration that such a man is bapitized, in communion with Rome, and possessing faith. But this would leave a great deal unsaid. Indeed, it would attract scarcely more than a politely indifferent nod of recognition. The Catholic is far more—and often far less.

In any exploration of meaning, we can always fall back on the traditional denotation of *catholic* by referring to the simple and inclusive term *universal*, which, upon some slight reflection, appears to mean very little. In an age that thrives more on connotations than on denotations, it might be more efficacious to analyze the term *catholic* for its

meaning within the framework of pluralism. This is necessary because Catholics don't live in a vacuum, nor do we
constitute the entirety of society. Rather, we are a part of
society.

Catholics, then, can be viewed from two perspectives,
from within and from without, and this has considerable
bearing on what description comes forth. Further and far
more important, it can help reveal the great breach that
exists between Catholics and non-Catholics. Also, we can
possibly learn a great deal from the other's description, and
out of this knowledge form a greater mutual understanding
that will help close the breach.

It is essential to accept the fact that each perspective
though terribly at odds with the other, is founded on sincere
conviction and not upon hostile suspicion or perverse ill-
will. The Catholic is what he is, while from another viewpoint he is only what he appears to be. And this is really the
basis of confusion. However, lest there be any misunderstanding, let me hasten to add that the Catholic, though he
is what he is, often confuses the reality of his nature with
what he imagines it to be. In an effort to sort all this out, I
would like to sketch two impressions of but a single identity, first from within and then from without.

What, then, of Catholicism and the Catholic?

The most startling thing about Catholicism is its liberating tendency—at least in theory. It doesn't bind the individual *against* something; it girds him *for* something. But
we are all, Catholic and non-Catholic, governed largely by
emotion, and hence logic and reason play a small role in
our lives. As I have said, our view of Catholicism is com-

plicated by the position from which we view it. There is nothing less inviting or attractive than the great stained windows of a cathedral when viewed from the outside; but what in Christendom is more magnificent than these same stained windows when seen from the inside, against the light of the sun? In brief, then, the Church is the starting point from which one ventures forth, not the dim object as seen from without.

The Catholic is no single thing, whether he is a cleric or layman. The key to understanding what is meant by *Catholic* is the realization that all Catholics are sinners. True, we may not each claim the same sort of sin, but providentially, God has given all of us ample scope for our individual talents. Your pride may be my covetousness, but nevertheless, there is more than enough to go around. Most of us, Catholic and non-Catholic, fail to recognize that the Catholic Church is composed of sinners. (God knows, it would be wonderful if it were otherwise, but then if it were, there would be no need for the Church.) What makes the Church unique, as we view it, is that it provides the means to salvation more efficaciously than does any principle outside the Church, in addition to the obvious fact that it was founded by God—but the second point is not apparent to those outside the Church. It was once fashionable to say that there was no salvation outside the Church, but that was only man's voice; God decrees otherwise. That saying embodies a terrible misconception—that only the Catholic Church provides a chance for salvation, that the native of Central Africa or Asia who never received instruction from a wandering Jesuit was doomed to hell simply because no one sprinkled water in a prescribed way and mumbled a cryptic Latin phrase. Salvation had nothing to do with the man's heart, only with an incantation. But God sees our hearts, not our sprinkled foreheads. Today, fortunately, we are more aware of our neighbors, and the only step left is to love them.

Since Catholics are sinners and since non-Catholics are not always depraved, where are we in our attempts at definition? The Catholic is a man—but a man with a difference. The Catholic, formal or otherwise, is aware of some terrible mystery that separates him from the beasts and yet also separates him from the angels. No man who ever *loved* perished; and yet the man who loves cannot penetrate the ineffable mystery that is love. He may yearn, he may feel a terrible absence, but the mystery remains. It is very much like the man who thirsts in the desert. He may not know the chemical composition of water or the physiological needs of the body; all he knows is that he thirsts. This is what makes a man Catholic: his awareness of his thirst. We become members of the Mystical Body (but then what of those who never hear of the well?) to quench this terrible thirst. Being what we are, however, we must return again and again to the well; otherwise we will perish. The well is sacramental; our thirst arises from our fallen nature.

But this does not identify the diversity that resides in unity. It fails to record God's infinite capacity to create. How can we explain the evils of history, the glorious sanctity of saints? Given simply, the Catholic is a man aware of the mysterious, but with varying perception and varying concern about that mystery. A man baptized has greater means at his disposal—if he will use them; a man unbaptized has fewer. This tenet of the faith we believe with a profundity that must never be misunderstood. Formal Catholics too often fail to recognize Christ's truth, that He came to save sinners, not saints. They confuse themselves with saints—all the rest are sinners.

Viewed legalistically, as I have said, the Catholic is one baptized, possessing faith, and in communion with Rome. While this legalism may be true, it fails to satisfy the dictates of the heart; it is narrow, precise, cold. If it is true that Christ came to save all mankind, it must be because of His love for all, not merely for those who fit within the legalistic terms of strict definition. What is cardinal is the salvation of all mankind, not merely of those within the gates. The Catholic, then, if definition is required, is *he who goes out* of the cathedral and into the market place. What possible mission can there be for those who remain within the limits of legalism? No authentic Catholic can really be Catholic unless he obeys the commission of our Lord and goes out to all peoples and all nations.

Every Catholic, then, is a missionary—or should be. But there are missionaries and missionaries. There is the one, so eloquently described by Thomas Merton, who carries Christ to the pagan, supremely convinced that he is bringing a stranger to the sinner, but who fails to realize that in meeting the pagan he is meeting Christ. The true missionary is he who carries Christ to Christ, in a spirit of love. To force the host on the tongues of strangers is to force a particle of dry matter on the tongue of Christ. What merit is there in ritual without love? And in Western history how much love has there been for the dirty savages who stare in wonder at their new god, the white stranger with his little round talisman?

The missionary must love that which he carries with him, and he must also, and to no lesser degree, love those to whom he comes. Every man has value, whether lord or vassal, pagan or priest. As formed by God and possessing an immortal soul, each is of *infinite* worth and infinitely precious to God, Who presides over him no less than He does over the saint. It is a common error to believe that everything Catholic is good and everything not Catholic is bad. The pagan is a sinner! But so is the Catholic. The Protestant, the atheist, the Communist—all are sinners! But so is the Catholic.

What, then, marks the Catholic so as to separate him from other sinners? Two things: the promises of Christ, and the sharing of those promises with all mankind, not in pride but in humility. In this state of being and in this flow of action we discover the true nature of the Catholic. Therefore, what is Catholic is universal. In fact and in potential all men are Catholic; that is why we must view all men as brothers, not one as superior and the other as inferior, not one as good and the other as bad. What is it all about, really? Simply the union of all souls with God through eternity. It is because we love one another that we seek the greatest good for one another; and that good consists of eternal happiness with God.

The Catholic quite sincerely believes he has a mission to bring all men to God, and this out of love. The difficulty, however, arises out of his general failure to reveal this love.

Too often the missionary effort is presented all wrong. The Catholic may be utterly convinced of his sincerity and the merit of his attempts, and will be honestly disturbed when his non-Catholic neighbor turns away. What is wrong, of course, is that the Catholic almost never sees himself the way others do. He needs a mirror.

Briefly, then, let us look at Catholics as they appear to others. And in doing this, I must confess to some measure of authority since I spent nearly the first thirty years of my life looking at Catholics from the outside, before finding myself compelled to enter the strange and almost mysterious society known as the Catholic Church.

The average layman, whenever we get a clear view of him, is hardly distinguishable from anyone else except that he doesn't eat meat on Friday, at least not unless a hostess' feelings are at stake, and that he goes to his church services every Sunday, or almost every Sunday. That is just about it.

Society, being distressingly polite as well as pluralistic, doesn't countenance bickering over religious niceties, so the Catholic's views on things aren't really known. It is rumored that Mary is given peculiar treatment and that priests don't marry. Of course, everyone has heard the nonsense that the pope claims to be infallible, but everyone also knows that this is absurd (if he is so clever, why doesn't he play the stock market?). If one enters a layman's home he will quite often see embarrassingly bad pictures that are meant to represent assorted saints and other mythical creatures, but courtesy prevents any comment, just as one ignores a *faux pas* at a cocktail party. There may be an occasional book or magazine but they are either so formidable-looking or so drab of cover that one never fingers them, to say nothing of reading a bit here and there. Conversation, say, at a barbecue will be general and languidly profane, and the food ordinary. There may be an unintentional slip about "Father Tobin" or "parochial school," or even about the bishop whose picture was in the local paper in connection with the latest controversy over birth control. Naturally, one restricts one's comments to the sweet expression on the bishop's face.

As the years pass and any number of laymen enter one's life, the general impression persists that they are all pretty much alike. And yet—there is a difference. It isn't so much what they do or say; it's more what they are. One can't put one's finger on it; it's too elusive. But still, there is some particle of difference. They don't seem any sadder or happier than anyone else. They have the same pleasures, the same experience with death, and not all their marriages are happy. What is it, anyway? Certainly, they aren't more sincere in their beliefs; after all, one's own beliefs are just as honest, just as much a part of one's life as those complex and mysterious principles professed by Catholics.

There is always this slightly jarring notion that there is *something* different; different, but necessarily better? That isn't very likely, but it does tend to explain their small conceits. That could be it, you know: they are quite sure of themselves even if they don't come right out and say so. No. That's entirely beside the point. It's more as if they know something others don't. Or is it? Catholics can be so damned unsettling. One can spend a lifetime among them and never be the wiser. In the end, one goes about one's business and forgets the whole thing, sometimes slightly oppressed, sometimes annoyed.

The priest, on the other hand, is an altogether different article. Everyone knows all about priests. They wear those dreary black suits and those silly stiff collars that no one else would think of wearing. They live alone in a large, dark house, their lives overseen by elderly housekeepers (rather discreet, that point of always insisting on old ladies who invariably resemble one's ancient aunt who lost her husband twenty years ago). Priests, of course, don't marry, which must be rather hard on the younger ones. There is more to it, however. Can a bachelor truly counsel couples about sex and that sort of thing? And doesn't it tend to make them, if one may be completely open, somewhat less than a man? Not a sissy, exactly, but still, *different?*

There are even times when one actually meets a priest, generally in a public place so that no more than a word or two of introduction passes between you. He seems quite ordinary up close. It is conceivable that a friend drags one to a church service on some pretext or other ("We can drive straight out to the golf course without losing the ten minutes over to your house."). In the church, one sees something that might have come directly from the Middle Ages. The priest has his back to you constantly, except when he lectures for a few minutes about a church fund drive or reads a letter from someone ("The Bishop," one's friend whispers) explaining that the mixed marriage is on the rise, constituting an increased danger to the sanctity of marriage, since it raises questions on birth control that

Catholics can answer in only one way. It's all very complicated and one loses the drift.

But the priest is there, all done up in layer upon layer of gowns, topped by some sort of ornate poncho that surely must have cost a fortune. The whole spectacle is odd. There are little picture plaques on the walls, and statues with candles—hundreds, it seems—burning in front of them. There is a railing that seems to cut the priest off from the people and a tablelike structure with any number of tall candlesticks that must have cost a fortune, too.

The service (when there isn't a lecture) is all in Latin,* which no one speaks any more and which no one studies for more than a year or so in order to get on in high school. What an odd practice, to do the whole thing in a language no one can understand. It makes one wonder. In all ways, it is a peculiar business, with the priest repeatedly washing his hands, filling a cup (with no more than a thimbleful), and—after all sorts of delays—drinking out of the cup and eating some kind of very thin wafer.

The people never sit still. They stand for a while, then sit, then kneel, then drop quickly to one knee and up again before one can think of what to do next. It may seem a betrayal of some secret, but more than a few actually read, not paying the least attention to what is going on. And, then there are those bells that jerk one out of reveries. Through it all, the priest keeps up his mumbling (what if he mumbled in English—would it make any difference?),

---

* When this was written Latin was the vogue. Since the institution of liturgical reforms a great deal of the Latin has been removed, although not entirely.

turning around briefly several times as if to check up on the people. Finally, after a burst of bells, a number of people get up and march to the railing and kneel. The priest puts something small (from a distance it is reminiscent of the candy wafers one ate as a child) in each open mouth, not once seeming to care that so few want what he has to give.

When it is all over one wonders what it was all about, this indifferent hour when no one knew what was being said and when nothing really happened and where almost no one seemed interested in the least. What could that service mean to anyone? Particularly when it is repeated every Sunday of the year? And those poor people are forced to make an appearance each and every Sunday of their lives until they die.

What an extraordinary thing, this church-going.

The priest, once in a great while, comes closer. It may be when he rings the doorbell to ask if any Catholics live there. He smiles politely and leaves when told no. Or it may be at a friend's house where, for the first time, one realizes the friend is Catholic and further that he has invited a priest to dinner, along with a number of other people. This may well be the only time a stranger and a priest will ever talk beyond polite introductions and equally polite farewells.

The ordinary thing would be cordiality, but how is one cordial with a priest? The hostess is at ease, offering the priest a drink, and the priest sets it down as he reaches for a cigarette. There are others about who chat aimlessly with the priest; some of the remarks are general, others seem almost a secret language (Arthur's first communion, Monsignor's requiem, C.C.D., etc., etc.). At one point, generally when one finds oneself seated next to the priest at dinner (after that momentary fumbling for words as the priest offers a blessing), the priest will turn and ask what one does. One suddenly realizes that these are the first words between them. One replies briefly and there is a strained silence since there's scarcely any need to return the question.

Observing the priest, one is quickly convinced that there is nothing unusual about him, except for a tendency to speak with a subtle hint of authority in all matters. When he favors something it is not unusual to see most of his audience readily agreeing; and when he becomes critical his criticism is quickly matched by that of his audience. He may tell a mild little story, but the laughter seems a bit out of proportion. One also observes that the priest is served first and that no one suggests leaving the table until after the priest has given ample evidence that he couldn't possibly eat another piece of cake or drink another cup of coffee. On the way out of the dining room the priest comments briefly but expansively on the fine quality of the hostess' food. One is then aware that for the second time one is tentatively engaged in conversation with a priest. But what does one say to a priest?

As if to break the tension, one stammers that one is not a Catholic; it sounds like an apology. The priest, smiling, remarks that he knows one's clergyman; in fact, they played golf just the other day. Rather disconcerted, one makes a limp confession of being a terrible golfer, to which the priest makes his own confession of inadequacy. And then there is silence between the priest and the stranger.

The priest leaves early, after a small cognac or a last cup of coffee. He shakes everyone's hand, and the hostess is particularly fervent in her expressions of pleasure at having had the priest in her home. For a few minutes everyone clamors to say how much they like the priest and what an outstanding job he has done in building the new church building and starting up the school. The only jarring note is someone's remark (the hostess pretends not to hear and one suspects the man has had a bit to drink) that he doesn't know how he can afford the pledge he has made for the new school; he was hardly able to contribute to the new church building.

However, contradicting the clamorous praise, there is a subtle change in the living room. It's as if everyone had been almost holding in a portion of his breath. Now people seem to breathe, possibly not more freely, but at least differently. The cognac is passed once more, and then a third time. It is late when one gets home, and the next morning there is the slightest suggestion of a hangover.

As to bishops, the ordinary stranger scarcely knows of their existence. An occasional picture appears in the local paper, but there are so many pictures that one passes the bishop by as he studies a photograph of an aspiring starlet posing rather indiscreetly to further her own career and the ambitions of some commercial association. One wonders if the bishop in question notices or is concerned over the juxtaposition. There are a few strangers who get to know the bishop very well, but rather as a business prospect than as an ecclesiastic.

Every stranger knows the pope, less as head of the

Catholic Church than as an Italian who is obviously both good copy and photogenic in an ancient and ornate way.

Pope Pius XII was thin and intellectual; Pope John XXIII was fat and friendly. Pope Paul VI is medium-sized and considerably younger than Pope John, who, as every stranger knows, convened a council that even strangers seemed to like. Why, no one knows, except that John thought it up and there was something about the man. It wasn't because he was a pope or because he was very old. It was something else, something too tenuous to put into words. What was it that made him different? He wasn't clever, he wasn't profound; he didn't do anything unusual. He didn't solve the world's problems. He was just an old man. And yet there was something about him.

If a stranger were to reflect upon the whole massive thing known as the Roman Catholic Church, the reflection might go as follows. The Church claims to be the largest single religious body in the world. It claims that Jesus established it in His lifetime, that it is the only true religion in the world, and that the popes are the legitimate successors of Peter, whom Jesus appointed to head up everything. The Catholic Church claims that the pope is infallible and that Mary is physically in heaven. For centuries the Church pretty much ran Europe as it wanted and became very corrupt. Thanks to Luther and a series of brave men, the Church was put in its place and was shown that two (or more) could play the same game.

Today, after centuries of competition, the Catholic Church is generally secure and claims a large membership. However, though rising in public favor, the Catholic

Church is still something of a mystery. To most strangers, it seems somewhat remote. It is like an enormous structure on the outskirts of a large city. And since this structure, planted so deep on its spot, can't move, one must travel out of town even to approach it. The Catholic Church is more of a private city than a part of the city it is so close to. Since it has all its own facilities and activities, it is conceivable that it could be quite cut off and still carry on undisturbed, or even unaware of the destruction of everything around it.

Every stranger knows something about the Catholic Church; but not very much. To the stranger, the Catholic Church is very unapproachable. Some even suspect it of conceit. One may travel quite a distance to inspect this enormous structure, but one does so almost entirely on one's own. True, there are posted signs that lead the way, but they are very small signs, widely spaced, and written in an almost undecipherable antique language. With so little encouragement, it is remarkable that strangers even try to approach it. Sometimes an occasional stranger will invite the Catholic Church to move closer into the city, but the answer is always a polite and firm "No." This obstinacy requires one to do things on their premises and in their framework of rules, that is, sign up for membership (revocable on their part and irrevocable on the member's part) or go away.

The Catholic Church has an opinion on everything. And there matters rest. Catholics talk a great deal to the rest of the world—rather like a broadcast from a remote hook-up —and continue living their own lives precisely as they did a thousand years ago. They moralize endlessly and have a very low opinion of others. This last business is disconcerting; they claim to know so very much about goings-on in a city they've never even entered. Though the Catholic Church is formally present in the twentieth century, it is really in the thirteenth, when everything was so pleasant, so Catholic. The Church is very old-fashioned and speaks very broken English.

The Catholic Church is an oddity, and yet it seems not to care that it has captured the modern popular fancy as an oddity rather than as an entity to be seriously considered— seriously as one considers the danger of thermonuclear war or the population explosion. The Catholic Church is often taken into men's considerations, but more as an obstructive force than as a participant in world events.

If a stranger can believe some of its spokesmen, the Church may have a uniqueness, but no one outside knows much about that. One only knows what one sees and hears and experiences.

The question is often asked, why have so many millions of people throughout the ages, especially in modern times when we know so much more, chosen to live in that confounding world apart known as the Roman Catholic Church? Why do they submit their wills to the directives of a man in Rome? Why do they show themselves so convinced that they are right and everyone else is wrong? Why their perverse refusal to bend for the common good? Why do they rail against divorce, artificial birth control, and abortion? Why do they have their own school system? Why do they insist on weekly attendance at mass? Why don't their priests marry?

The questions reflect the mystery of the Church—the mystery the rest of the world ponders both seriously and with exasperation. *There is something about the Church,* and no stranger can put his finger on exactly what it is.

Only a Catholic can dispel the mystery. Only the Church can explain itself and answer the world's questions. What is this something that makes the layman, priest, bishop, and pope?

Catholics sense this mystery to varying extents. Some cannot put it into words; they know only that if they were to go away from it, they would never feel right. Something would be missing; what exactly they couldn't say, but they would sense it. Others can talk about the true holiness of the Church, its unique and divine origins, the sustenance of the Holy Spirit, the promises of Christ. They can point to the many saints and miracles, the unbroken line from Peter to Paul VI, and the martyred witnesses to the faith.

They can do all this and yet not move a single heart. Once they could. The Church's greatest glory came to it in those dangerous centuries when imperial Rome straddled the world and Christianity was a fragile whisper that if overheard could send the Christian to torture and death. And when it wasn't death that claimed the Christian, it was laughter or indifference. But the Christian persisted and won.

This is an awesome heritage that is held in common by all Christians, not merely Catholics. And yet, despite this, there is grave estrangement between Catholics and the rest of Christendom today. The fault doesn't lie with one or the other exclusively; we bear a common obligation to discard the impediments to understanding and reconciliation.

Whereas it would be presumptuous for a Catholic to call upon non-Catholics to do away with their defects, it is fully within the competence of that same Catholic to suggest that his family set about the task of hard introspection with the aim of action—action that will erase the almost disastrous image he projects to the rest of society. But we must do more than erase an image; we must change certain realities—from within.

5 ❧

INTERMEZZO

TOO many Americans appear to be utterly surprised to hear the Negro protest against evils that have plagued his existence for centuries. These Americans, so long immersed in indifference, imagine that the Negro has just now found his voice, not for an instant realizing that the Negro has been crying out for generations. What makes the present moment in our national history unique is that the white man is at last beginning to listen. The greatest danger we face is that we may merely listen and refuse to do anything more.

The same thing is true of the so-called emerging voice of the layman. Interestingly enough, while the Negro protest has been with us for a long time, the layman has just barely begun to express his feelings. There is always risk in speaking after centuries of silence, the risk that one's audience may first take offense at the uninvited speech and then not be willing honestly to listen. The greatest menace to Negro aspirations, as I just said, is that the massive white voice will answer the Negro plea for recognition with a resounding "No!" For the white to do this would be to court national disaster. Similarly, for the clerical segment of the Church to turn a deaf ear to the voice of the layman, or worse, to attempt to forge a future for the Church in antiquated terms that exclude the layman, would be to court disaster for the Church.

We are in the process of breaking with the past in order to form a more viable future. But part of this process as adumbrated in all that Vatican II is doing, will inevitably be a break in old relationships. Earlier I described the development of new alignments that include both laity and clergy in the two contending camps. It would be futile to conclude that those who clamor for a vigorous readjustment of the Church's perspective are in the majority, particularly with regard to relational difficulties between clergy and laity. While we have clerics like Cardinal Cushing, Archbishop Roberts, Hans Küng, and Thomas Merton, who clearly belong to the new wave of clerical thinking, we have far more cardinals and bishops and priests who want nothing less than clerical supremacy (as distinguished from mere ascendancy) and lay servitude. To their way of thinking, the laity are a serious impediment to the Church and are tolerated simply because they are the fertilized field that produces the flower of Catholicism, the clergy. And in the same vein, there are far too many laymen who, being completely indifferent to Church affairs, would prefer that things remain as they have been for centuries. To their way of thinking the Church, with its demanding clergy, is a serious impediment to their secular ambitions and is tolerated simply because there is no alternative.

However, the future of the Church must be prepared for regardless of the forces which look longingly to the past. The key to this preparation lies in the termination of old alliances and the formation of new ones. Rather than extend the traditional practice of clerical activity and lay passivity, thus perpetuating the principle of alienation by classification, we must align ourselves along ideological lines. This will have a consequence which cannot be ignored: that *ideas,* regardless of source, will determine a particular circumstance and even a course of action. Fundamental in every case will be the acceptance of active lay participation in the affairs of the church. This, of course, will be anathema to the rigid separatists; it will be a balm to others.

It is not in the scheme of things Catholic that the layman take command of the Church. But then, the layman doesn't want that to happen any more than does the most reactionary cleric. Not to be the least bit facetious, the layman wouldn't take the vows if the pope himself asked. The layman, as well as the cleric, is fully aware of the role of God's grace in vocations; just as the cleric has his, the layman has his God-given vocation. What is meant by active lay participation in the affairs of the Church is that the layman wishes to offer what he has to give, in response not to clerical inducement but to that internal voice which calls all men to help a loved one. And here the loved one is the Church universal.

Because we live in an age that thrives on externals, the

temptation is always present to leap into the areas of discussion that are concerned with structural and organizational details. It seems that whenever a problem arises the solution suggested is to organize a committee that will engage in some inchoate activity. This is not appropriate to our situation today. What is needed far more urgently is reflection, but not clerical reflection on clerical words. The word of the layman must form the basis for true reflection. Only in this way will something new and vital be injected into Catholic thought.

Probably the most basic additive needed in Catholic thought is the concept of mutuality. This concept must end the centuries-old tradition of thinking in terms of lay and clerical separation, as if it were the consequence of the distinction of identities. In the broadest sense, we are all equal members of the Mystical Body of Christ; our equality simply takes different forms. That is, we basically divide between the clerical form (and here I include all religious ways of life that are founded on special vows) and the lay.

Where we have always had our difficulties is over the matter of clerical authority, which seems at times to be more dictatorial than fraternal. This, I suspect, arises from a misconception shared by the laity and the clergy. We tend to consider the matter of authority without looking carefully at authority to discover whether there is something behind it. Actually, we see the situation more or less in reverse. What truly marks the clergy is their voluntary assumption of responsibility. From *this* stems authority. It would be the rankest folly to allow a man to accept certain

responsibilities without granting him the authority he must
have to meet them. It would be like telling the head of a
household, who has assumed the obligations of supporting
his family, that we deny him the means of earning a living.

The situation in the Church is not unlike that of American society in general (despite everything said heretofore
about the Negro), in which all citizens, at least theoretically, have certain inalienable rights and are equal before
the law. As part of citizenship, there are certain basic re-
quirements for conduct that form the minimal obligations
everyone must assume. Essentially, these are that we obey
the laws of the community. However, if someone voluntarily assumes added responsibility by accepting some office
which exists for the good of the community, he *must* be
granted the authority to promote that good. Whether we are
talking of a town councilman or the President, the basic
principle holds true, and an increase in responsibility necessarily carries with it an increase of authority.

Within the Church, the ultimate source of authority is
God's law. And the authority of the clergy comes from this.
However, we must not lose sight of the reason for this authority: responsibility. Where we have all gone astray is in
failing to appreciate the antecedent responsibility. This is a
common fault. We all rather enjoy authority and the power
it gives us. Responsibility, on the other hand, tends to be a
terrible inconvenience to our achieving personal ends.
What marks responsibility is service to others; what marks
authority is service to ourselves. This is true not only of the
clerical situation; it is the secret that explains the general
lack of lay interest in the Church. We prefer making our

meager fortunes in the market place to serving something outside of ourselves.

Fortunately, this selfishness is beginning to give way to something better. But only a beginning has been made, and it should not be the basis of conceit on anyone's part.

So we are distinct but one within the Church. We each have our various functions and our various responsibilities. Everything else is detail. What is not detail is mutual love, something that has not been very apparent for a long time. In the early days it was said, "See how the Christians love one another." We must bring that saying up to date.

The layman seeks to speak, on the basis of mutuality of interest as well as mutuality of dignity. This is a legitimate aspiration, particularly in the modern age that sees so many laymen intellectually quite mature. Without being clannish about it, I will point out that many laymen are the intellectual superiors of many of the clergy. In the spirit of Christian ecumenism, I must also add that vast multitudes of the laity are the intellectual inferiors of much of the clergy. But once past the matter of mental rivalry, what are we to do with the intelligence contained in the Church?

Quite obviously, we must use our talents, regardless of who possesses what particular competence. This principle, I am afraid, is going to cause all sorts of difficulties among those who can't quite accept lay opinion on anything more exalted than economic manipulation or political chicanery. But if the Church and society are to be served, they must be served by more than one mind.

The greatest mistake the clergy could possibly make would be to place competent lay minds in an inferior status, handing out assignments to the laity much as a teacher hands out homework to school children. What is needed is a genuine coming together of equals who respect each other's competence. Ascendancy must be discarded or the Church will suffer an irreplaceable loss, because the intellectual layman will no longer accept whatever meager crumbs are offered him. Instead, he will lend his talents elsewhere. Going it alone is no longer a luxury the clergy can afford, but they will go it alone unless they replace the conceit of paternalism with the humility of fraternity.

The first and probably most significant change that must occur in clerical thinking is toward the Catholic community itself. We are long past the age of the "Bingo priest" who can amuse (and enrich) his parish with a communal game. The philosophy behind such a condescending attitude is: paying the bills can be fun. The modern Catholic is beyond the candy stage of development and bitterly resents being spoken down to.

This is actually an extraordinary situation. All week long we live a most complex existence that makes enormous intellectual demands on us; then on Sunday we too often sit in our pews listening to a priest discourse on trivia. We are told that we should love our neighbor, that we shouldn't cheat in business, that children should honor their parents, that we should read the local Catholic newspaper, and that we should not practice artificial birth control.

If we are not told that sort of thing, we are encouraged to join all the parish organizations, the thought being that if we cling closely enough together in some ridiculous parish grouping we will somehow be better for it. It is analogous to that insipid slogan, "The family that prays together stays together," as if the practice of mutual prayer will act as a magical mending tape on the family fabric.

And then there is the matter of spiritual guidance, which is so conspicuously absent in the confessional, where everyone rushes through the action with one eye on the long line waiting. So intent are we all on the long line that if someone stays beyond his brief moment, we all wonder what endless stream of crimes he has committed. We find the whole matter very embarrassing.

So we have sermons and penance. There is little else of a spiritual nature—at least in common experience. Those few who want something beyond the ordinary child's diet must seek out that rare soul who can speak above a spiritual whisper. The rest of us, it pains me to say, subsist on spiritual dregs. We have the sacraments and our limited understanding of them but almost nothing else.

A most serious flaw in Church management is the practice of appointing bishops who are noted for being good administrators. If there is one thing a bishop *shouldn't* be, it's a good administrator; he should be the holiest man available. After all, good administrators can be hired by the scores, whereas we have far too few holy men to lead the Church in its earthly mission. No bishop will go to heaven because he ran an efficient organization; he will go there if he is holy. Being an administrator is essentially a technical matter; holiness is not quite the same thing. Also, there is a danger that an Administrator-Bishop will be rather taken by his organizational genius, to the sacrifice of his true responsibility: the salvation of souls.

Just as we have efficient bishops, so we also have efficient pastors who see the parish more as a business venture than as a spiritual responsibility. Of course, we recognize the need for *things* within the Church; we realize that there is a social aspect to the faith that involves schools, church buildings, hospitals, and all the rest. But must we always be told about these things without the least clerical effort to incorporate us into the various schemes, beyond the mere fact of being informed that we will have to foot the bills?

The Church is in an economic crisis. Or rather, the Church isn't in the crisis; the layman is. The clergy, long supported and personally innocent of economic realities, rush so enthusiastically into a well-constructed future that they never seem aware of the painful economic facts which accompany every new apostolic building and program. A parish needs a school or the diocese needs a new seminary. With a naïveté more appropriate to a cloistered order, the bishop holds out his checkbook, ready for the layman's signature. We are reputed to be an affluent society, but we also go a long way toward supporting much of the world. We have our church bills to pay, but we have a whole host of taxes as well. This is no place to set forth a family budget, but it is the place to protest the almost cavalier demands for more, more, and more money. We simply don't have it.

It would help if the clergy took counsel with knowledgeable laymen who have had the trying experience of meeting a payroll. While the clergy possess a childlike faith in the lay economic subsidy, the average layman has no such comforting assurance. Employees and tax agencies don't care a rap about one's good intentions; they demand cash on the barrel head. Under such stern circumstances the layman has learned the value of a dollar. He also knows about meeting obligations and planning his affairs in order to do so. He does not enjoy the luxury of faith in someone else's good will or forgiveness. It has been said that a pope can always sign a blank check and have it honored. This is not true for the layman, and yet he is called upon to pay for everything in the Church from a great cathedral through the vestments the priest wears at mass to the very food eaten in the rectory. Naturally, we wish to serve needs, but I am afraid the blank check is a thing of the past. We need an accounting—not after the fact but before, with the layman being consulted, for once.

There are two facets to this problem that must be stated and understood separately: pure economics and attitude. Economically, the layman is hard put to support a recklessly expanding Catholic economy, and even if he could, he doesn't like being told to pay for this or that without even the slightest effort to consult him. Until those who formulate Catholic expansionist policies begin to change traditional practices, they are going to find themselves confronted by increasing resistance, which will eventually become refusal. Of course, there are those who will chalk this up to obstinacy and covert anti-Catholicism, but they will be completely wrong.

The solution lies in respecting the layman, particularly in an area that is so much more within his competence than the priest's, by working out these matters with him. If this is done, not only will the Church go far in ordering its economic life, but the tendency to break down the walls of

separation will be reinforced. The latter is terribly important because resentment often closes a purse. We give only
so much, knowing that tomorrow will present its own demands. And there are so many tomorrows.

Modern society is so complex that no single person or
group can grasp either its essentials or its manifold terms in
a single experience. The clergy spend their formative years
preparing for but one particle of the whole. They are
trained in their specialty much as a physicist is trained in
his. But physics isn't the entirety of science. And formal
religious training is not capable of embracing all of life. It
might appear that the solution would be to lengthen seminary training in an effort to increase the individual priest's
scope. But this would not solve our problems. The point is
that no single person can learn all there is to learn; all the
varied experiences must be shared, including within the
Church. But if we are going to do this, we must begin with
certain basic assurances that will lead to a genuine sharing.

To begin with, the clergy will need to accept greater responsibility for their own thinking. Too often do priests
seem to want to leave everything up to God and the good
will of the laity. A priest utterly ignorant of reality will rely
on God to explain such realities as politics, psychology, anti-
Catholicism, evolution—all the problems that demand investigation, not prayed-for revelation, for their solution. Or
again, the laity are frequently relied on to provide comforting answers to clerical questions; the priest wants to be
reassured that what he stands for is right. To this end, fearful of the worst, he wants reality bent to fit his convenience.
This fear, of course, arises out of his ignorance of so much

of our complex society, which is the unhappy result of his lack of opportunity to investigate reality, coupled with his mistrust of the lay mind which has absorbed experience but which might not possess sufficient Catholicity to place everything under the protective umbrella of religious orthodoxy. This largely explains why Catholic education is both so timid about experimentation and so completely dominated by the clergy.

The widespread lack of thought we suffer from today is a terrible hangover from all that intellectual tyranny founded upon Trent. And it is precisely this tyranny which must be done away with if the Church is to participate in the affairs of contemporary society. While a few tentative efforts are being made to break with this dismal intellectual past, the bulk of Catholic intellectualism is still harnessed to an orthodoxy that *a priori* suspects novelty, change, and anything else which upon the most cursory examination gives some hint of religious difficulty. If it is correct that all truth is one, then there should be no fear of whatever we come across. Truth, however unpleasant, is not error.

The layman, being so much a part of society as well as of the Church, lives with novelty, change, and religious difficulty, as it fills his experiential life. Despite clerical discouragement, he has gone into the delicate areas of sociology, psychology, science, the arts, and all the other disciplines that cry out for reconciliation with traditional patterns of religious thought. And he has found that the reconciliation is very easily made. Indeed, there is really no need for "reconciliation"; all that is needed is understanding and just a bit of faith that God is the originator of all things, whether a subatomic particle or dream symbolism.

We have serious difficulty in all aspects of modern Church life in expressing ourselves forthrightly and unself-consciously. Too often we need to look to some imprimatur before we can speak out. We have lost spontaneity, and consequently we have lost the ability to love spontaneously. We are too fearful. We are too deep within the reserve of our mental fortress to contact the world around us. So intent are we on rigid orthodoxy that we fail to see anything else. In effect, we have become silent—all of us, not merely the laity. The clergy are silent about the subjects beyond the inner keep of the most stringent orthodoxy. They await liberation from this dungeon of silence. Perhaps, just perhaps, the layman holds the key that will open the door through which the clergy and the laity, as brothers, will walk into the future.

6 ❖

EDUCATION: THE CATHOLIC DILEMMA

WITHOUT doubt, the most serious and immediate problem of the Catholic Church in America is education. Over the years we have constructed a complex which rivals, in a very modest way, the secular and state systems. We have poured billions of dollars into our effort to provide every Catholic boy and girl with a Catholic education, beginning at the primary level and ending with advanced university degrees. Whole orders of nuns, brothers, and priests have dedicated their lives to running and staffing our thousands of schools. Generations upon generations of students have received their complete education "under one roof." And yet, the entire complex is on the verge of collapse, not only economically but philosophically as well.

Practically every Catholic is aware of the crisis that faces Catholic education, but no one seems able to come up with an answer. We are in a dilemma—actually two dilemmas.

The first is concerned with the economics of Catholic education, and the second with the very concept itself. Before we can resolve these dilemmas, we must first take a hard look at the realities of the situation.

Catholic education is neither "Catholic" nor "education." It is restrictive and retrogressive, the antithesis of growth. It is narrowly parochial and militantly antagonistic to all things non-Catholic. Above all, the system is founded on fear—a fear of things non-Catholic. And out of this fear, the Catholic Church in America has formed a Frankenstein's monster that threatens to turn its creators out into the street, bankrupt financially and philosophically.*

From a slightly different standpoint, Catholic education consists in erecting a mental fortress to protect its virginity. Anxious nuns and priests, aided and abetted by equally anxious parents, cloister not only the persons of the children but their minds as well. All things Catholic are good; all non-Catholic things are bad. From the unctuous primers that show John and Judy perched on our Lord's knee to university curricula that enthrone the legalistic syllogism, the Catholic intellect is wrapped in swaddling clothes. Its voice can only be raised in a recitation of Catholic shibboleths or a defensive bluster against those heretical "others" who threaten Catholic intellectual complacency. For every point raised outside the keep there are a hundred clerical voices chanting—in office—"Anathema!" Catholic

---

* Although I am, at the present time, advocating retention of the Catholic educational system (albeit, subject to profound reorientation), I am cognizant of the fact that a growing number of education specialists within the Church consider the system philosophically superfluous and financially impossible. Many recommend abandonment of the entire system.

education consists primarily in answers, but unfortunately they are answers without questions. In a way, Catholic education became fixed when St. Thomas Aquinas wrote what by his own designation was a prelude of his thoughts, a primer, if you will. From that day on, for over seven hundred years, Catholic education has suffered from hardening of the intellectual arteries.

The reason for this deadening proclivity is that education, particularly in the last few centuries, has become a means to an end, that is, a defense of the faith. Truth, standing alone, is completely irrelevant; what matters is a stout defense of Rome against the moral and intellectual barbarians of the North. A Protestant—or even worse, a Jew—may have something rather intelligent to say on a given subject, but his text gathers dust in a censor's office, generally with the pages uncut, while some loyal drone offers his own smiling simplicities that firmly and resolutely prove the utter perfection of thirteenth-century concepts. What a delightful reassurance it is to know:

> All men are rational animals.
> But, John is a man.
> Therefore, John is a rational animal.

I am sure John and the clever mind that forms more pliable minds are both relieved to hear such pleasant news, but that scarcely qualifies them for a degree.

The Catholic Church takes pleasure in having St. Thomas Aquinas on its side; it absolves all Catholics from thinking for themselves. One never need wrestle (as all others must) with abstruse and recondite questions; one merely has to see what the Angelic Doctor had to say and then plagiarize. Or if the venerable saint is too much, or unavailable, one can always go to a Jesuit for the answer and he will dust off a relic of the past, offering it as the final solution to present difficulties. This, of course, points out one of the central failings of Catholic education: it looks to the past, never to the future. In the past lies certainty (or so it seems); in the future lies uncertainty; and any institution on the defensive, seeking to preserve its pristine purity, must rest upon certainty. The result may be barrenness, but it is safe.

Another frailty of Catholic education is its habit of invoking God at every turn. No one can pursue a scientific thought without feeling a tap on the shoulder and hearing a clerical voice whisper, "That molecule was made by God." No psychologist may explore the psyche without some Roman collar pointing out that "God gave man free will." The paleontologist may seek out the origins of man, but his tent must carry a banner reading, "God gave man an immortal soul." The historian, weaving his way into the past, must also keep one eye on the dictum that "The Gnostics, Nestorians, Jansenists, Protestants, Jews, Moslems—all those others—have always been wrong, lock, stock and barrel, 100 percent of the time." Numbers are all right as long as the classroom bows before the number 3. The arts are perfectly acceptable as long as they confine themselves to morality plays and holy pictures.

It is terribly like a tender love scene where the hero, chastely pressing the fingertips of the nearly fainting ingénue, whispers gently, "I love you, my dear—but of course I love God more."

St. Augustine, in what many modern Catholics must consider a moment of madness, once said, "Love God, and then do as you please." This remarkable liberating sentiment has been replaced with the abomination, "Love God, and then do as *we* please." This could stand as the motto of Catholic educators in America.

Precisely, what is the situation? Catholic education is an institution within an institution, one school system within another. This other, unfortunately, is considered hostile— not relatively hostile but absolutely. We are instructed in this country that it is our duty as parents to send our children to parochial schools insofar as they are available. And every effort and dollar are being devoted to making total enrollment possible, even if it means economic ruin. There is something gallantly quixotic about a poor harried minority's challenging the vastness of America, making terrible sacrifices to fulfill an inherited dream.

The fact is we are hoist by our own petard. And it hurts.

There is no question that the great majority of Catholic parents want their children to have a Catholic education. At least, they do in the beginning, before they have experienced the *fact* of Catholic education. There is something very reassuring about fitting the child into a uniform (it *is* drab and a bit too large in places, but the child will grow into it). And there is the comforting thought that Father's influence will guard the school, much as the Holy Ghost guards the Church. The nuns in their quaint and curious habit, so dedicated, so humble, will help the child grow in wisdom, especially Catholic wisdom.

Even the books the child carries home are a solace; they are so *devotional*—pictures of smiling boys and smiling girls smiling at smiling priests and smiling nuns. There are even a smiling dog and a smiling cat smiling at everyone smiling smiles. Jesus and Mary and Joseph, maybe even a bishop or two, enter the pictorial lives of the children. Arithmetic problems are devotional: if John says seven Hail Mary's and Judy says three Hail Mary's, how many Hail Mary's do both John and Judy say? Or if there is a spelling bee, high on the list are such devotional words as *Father, Sister, bishop, pope, Church, rosary, mass, Gospel, vocation, religion, altar, apostle,* et cetera, et cetera. Needless to say, history is devotional and science is devotional. Added to all this, they have lessons in doctrine as well, which is clearly a case of carrying coals to Newcastle.

This is not education; it is indoctrination. The schools are not trying to educate children; they are trying to mold Catholics—and the particular mold used should never have been made, but given its creation, it should have been thrown away a century or more ago. Catholic elementary schools are called *parochial,* a most apt term to describe an education system that seeks but one end: a loyal, slightly literate aspirant for Catholic high school. Only such an extension of the parochial concept can take him. Finally, this prepared substance slips into a Catholic college, not to complete the molding—that has already been done—but only to round off the edges, to put on the final touches of sociological parochialism that will lead the graduate into a postgraduate ghetto of Catholic neighborhoods and parish suppers.

The purpose of this education system, as I said, is not to educate but only to produce good Catholics, safe Catholics, who will meld into a community, silent, obedient, supportive, with minds capable of reading with passable facility both the Sunday missal and the diocesan newspaper. The result of such an education process is to produce not excellence but acquiescent mediocrity.

In the elementary—and in most parochial—schools, one competes for sanctity by buying pagan children (God, what presumption!) and by seeing how many daily masses one can attend—all to be reported by a show of hands—in support of the month of Mary or the school's basketball team. Naturally, the child who fails to raise his hand, for whatever reason, is both humiliated and proven spiritually indifferent. In too many schools the cult of personality flourishes, with the presiding nun receiving homage quite regularly in the form of pageants, poems, paeans, and pronouncements; she sits, installed, while lisping children present themselves, curtsying, bowing, even genuflecting, in homage. Classrooms remain idle while children play games for Sister's pleasure.

Catholic education suffers from two serious drawbacks: a lack of funds and a lack of direction. While so much attention is being paid to the former, because it is so obvious, very little is paid to the latter, despite the fact that it is far more significant. Indeed, solve the latter and most assuredly the former would disappear. No one minds sacrifice if it may achieve some worthwhile result. But as things are, we have thousands of Catholic schools, elementary, secondary, and college, sadly lacking in worthiness.

To begin with, Catholic education as currently practiced is still clinging to antiquated practices and prejudices that are no longer applicable. The practice consists of marshaling boys and girls into a schoolyard ghetto and raising them intellectually separated from the rest of society. Boys and girls emerge from this system completely unprepared to face a non-Catholic idea or opinion. They have spent years —all their academic life—being spoon-fed a distorted view of all that exists outside the ghetto. Too, so much effort is spent on indoctrination that the true educational disciplines suffer from serious neglect, to such an extent that as students go to higher studies, they enter colleges and universities distinctly inferior to those outside the Catholic enclosure. A humiliating example of this may be found in the fact that students on all levels who want an *education,* including both priests and laymen who want to do serious graduate work, have to leave Catholic schools and study in secular universities. Further embarrassment—because it is so patently true—arises in any discussion with non-Catholic educators, who by and large can scarcely conceal their contempt for Catholic education, especially college-level and beyond.

One of the most distinctive qualities of the Catholic school on every level is its clannishness. Schools visit each other in mock rivalry, and form athletic leagues to keep good Catholic athletes together, uncontaminated by secularistic athletic ideology. There are Catholic all-American teams, all-city Catholic teams, the Catholic athlete of the year, Catholic girl bowling teams, and parish teams. Even in sports Catholics must huddle together.

All this indoctrination, this clannishness, this huddling together are based upon antiquated prejudices.

For generations the Catholics in America were an uncomfortable minority, surrounded by a hostile Protestant, Anglo-Saxon, puritanical majority, and had pretty much to protect themselves and yet not offend others. Also, the Church generally was in a defensive mood after Luther. It was in the spirit of the times to defend the faith. At the same time, and in this defensive mood, Catholics decided to withdraw from public education because it superficially mingled a bit of Protestant (and therefore amorphous) Bible reading and occasional Protestant homilies with the more formal education processes. Fearful of corruption, the Catholics set up their own system. Note that their purpose wasn't and still isn't to provide education but to protect their children from non-Catholic religious influences. And this is the prime error of the Catholic education system.

Ironically, today there would be no religious need for a separate system since the public schools have been systematically stripped of even the slightest religious taint. Therefore, the simplest solution to our present economic plight would be to enroll Catholic children in the antiseptic public schools and let the taxes paid by us all be put to the use of us all. Mind you, I am talking of education, not religious instruction, which is another matter. But does religious perspective have any place in teaching such fundamentals as reading, writing, arithmetic, basic science, basic history, and composition?

The above suggestion is actually only rhetorical in order to underline the basis for the separate Catholic school system: it was created for religious, not educational, purposes. As a result, the teaching is oriented more toward religious persuasion than toward intellectual development. It is more important that the child develop a "Catholic mentality" than his intellect.

This state of mind, this confusion, must end. But it can only end when our historic defensive posture gives way to religious confidence and respect for things non-Catholic. The Catholic must stop being afraid, as if exposure would destroy his beliefs. If his faith is so vulnerable, if the Church were a sham, a gross deception, then the ghetto would be needed to preserve the fantasy. But if the Resurrection was true, if Christ founded His Church on the Rock, then there is no vulnerability to alien ideas; rather, the Catholic, in his deep conviction, should welcome them so that the false may be so shown and the true added to the great store of Catholic truth.

There is another basic weakness in the Catholic system of education. It is controlled, administered, and largely staffed by nonprofessionals. By this I mean that despite specific training given various priests and nuns, their primary vocation is not to teaching but to either the priesthood or the sisterhood. When choosing a vocation, each has a choice: to dedicate himself to God or to teach. By entering the priesthood or an order, each makes a decision on a vocation. *Secondarily* they become teachers and administrators. Of course, some may conceive of this as a sort of double-barrel vocation, but that is trying to have your cake and eat it too; it simply won't wash.

In contrast to these are the men and women whose primary vocation is teaching. Just as the priest has his primary dedication to his vocation, so has the teacher to his. A good teacher, like a good priest, is totally dedicated. How else explain why some choose a profession in which everyone is underpaid, overworked, and unrespected by the community? There is talk of raising salaries, and yet many commentators are really hesitant; to place monetary incentive in the picture is to risk having people enter the profession for the money, not the vocation. It would be like making the priesthood a well-paying job, with the obvious danger of having money attract ambitious young seminarians to a lucrative future. Isn't this simply unthinkable of a priest and of a teacher?

Very few appreciate the sacrifices made by teachers. There are the obvious and very real ones, such as a surrender to a lifetime of marginal economic security, with the average teacher making much less money than most factory workers; and the problems of tenure and large work schedules. Probably hardest to bear is the indifference of the vast majority of both the students and the general populace. In such an anti-intellectual nation as ours, it is a term of opprobrium to call someone an intellectual.

And yet, the teacher bears all this. Why? Because he has a vocation—this business of knowledge, the vital *need* to pass it on, to see minds (even if only a few) develop. There is a truth, whether it is a sum of numbers or a subtle nuance in Milton, that *must* be seen. The fire of the teacher in his vocation is the same as the fire of the priest in his. Every day teachers hear of better-paying jobs, jobs less demanding, with a better future, offering more leisure time for family life; and yet they stay on. It would be a senseless thing to do unless there were the vocation.

The Catholic education system, founded on religious fear and not on a primary desire to provide education, has followed its religious inclination by placing the system in the charge of those with a religious vocation. Thus, while offering religious coloration, the Catholic Church has produced a third-rate education system. This is not to say that the priests and nuns are not really concerned with education; they merely lack the true vocation. They are distracted by eternity, and nothing temporal can be quite so important.

On the other hand, to the teacher it is. Under the present system, a priest is also a teacher. Similarly, there are times when a teacher is, say, a faculty advisor to the chess club; he may enjoy the game a great deal, but the time spent as an advisor results in a sacrifice of his time and attention to his true profession. It makes him less a teacher. So it is with the priest or nun who with one vocation engages in a secondary one. Can any priest or nun feel the same fire over a point of scholarship as they can feel over the sacrifice of the mass or marriage to the Spiritual Bridegroom?

Thus, we have a double basis for the inferiority of Catholic education: improper orientation toward religious isolation, and direction by nonprofessionals. There is a third basis, but it arises only in terms of higher education.

In the early years, when it is not essential, great emphasis is placed on the religious coloration of all educational activities, with an attendant diminution of intellectual disciplines. In a sense, this system is designed more to foster vocations to the priesthood and sisterhood than to prepare laymen for advanced education and ultimately for society. Indeed, one wonders if that isn't really what it's all about. Paradoxically, once the student enters college, there is an abrupt about-face. Prior education directed everything to God; now in college, everything is directed to secular success (although social ghettoism and dogmatic attitudes on non-dogmatic matters are encouraged)—and with a vengeance, as if Catholics, aware of earlier errors, were now determined not only to overcome the lapses of the past but to outdo the secularists.

Before proceeding, however, a distinction must be made between the cloistered finishing schools run by obscure orders whose sole purpose is to produce Catholic Junior Leaguers and the more serious colleges that have a somewhat more exalted purpose. Statistically the finishing schools are great in number, small in registration, rather expensive, and almost totally unproductive. One cannot discuss education seriously with regard to such institutions. Of far greater significance to the present discussion are the colleges that actually strive for accreditation, that actually have various undergraduate schools and even occasionally graduate schools, and that try to stress studies over social amenities; in other words, colleges that are actually trying to do something.

Unfortunately, they are mostly trying to do the wrong thing.

From an overall view, elementary education should be "Catholic *education,*" and college education should be "*Catholic* education." Naturally, we've managed to turn it all around. (Again, I am talking about education, not religious instruction.) The point is that the earlier student should be learning the techniques and the fundamental *facts* of life in order to apply them some day. He cannot do so when the education system is founded upon a desire for religious isolation. But what about application? Under our present system, the Catholic college doesn't take developed minds for the purpose of producing truly educated Catholics; it takes them to produce Catholic secularists.

This, then, raises the question as to what Catholic colleges should be. To begin with, they should not be technical schools training businessmen, scientists, lawyers, doctors and such, which is precisely what they are. Essentially, Catholic colleges suffer from me-too-ism: they have looked over other American colleges, liked what they saw, and set out to imitate them to the best of their impoverished ability.

What they have failed to see is that the other American colleges have no choice but to produce technicians, since pluralism proscribes a philosophical or religious orientation in education. And further, they have failed to see that the unique thing Catholics have *is* a philosophical and religious orientation that could be used to help Christianize American society. Instead they have built factories trying to compete with M.I.T., Stanford, Harvard, and the University of California—all this with almost no money. Economically, the Catholics simply can't pull it off. The result is a great number of also-rans that make the Catholic community the poor relations of American higher education.

What possible difference does it make whether chemistry is taught by a Jesuit or a Jew on a secular campus? Is there such a thing as "Catholic engineering," "Catholic biology," "Catholic law"? Do economic theories or the study of business cycles differ in Catholic and non-Catholic presentation? Pathology is simply pathology, and neither priest nor Protestant can alter the fact. While these are worthwhile disciplines, they have no religious connotations whatsoever, and should not be the dominant disciplines in Catholic higher education. And this for two reasons: first, we can't afford it, and second, Catholic colleges have a far greater contribution to make than as weak carbon copies of secular institutions.

The unique thing we have to offer America is our Catholicity. And Catholicity can best express itself in the area of liberal arts and the humanities. Science, business, law, and medicine can best be described as insensitive disciplines, in contrast to philosophy, literature, history, psychology, and sociology, which are sensitive disciplines. By *sensitive* I mean disciplines in which both the teacher and the student must bring into play their own perspective, their own philosophy of life, at almost every turn. A mathematical formula is just that, but an understanding of Kant, an interpretation of Camus, the relevance of Luther to modern history, the forces that motivate hostility, the understanding of social forces—all require a philosophical context in which to be placed. It is in these sensitive disciplines that Catholic colleges could play a tremendous part in modern society. It is here that the emphasis should be placed—where it counts.

Unfortunately, Catholics have not done this. In fact, they have by and large tended to play down these subjects, especially as contrasted with many of the insensitive disciplines that they have encouraged—to the brink of financial disaster. There is a further advantage to realigning the emphasis: cost. The disciplines that really are appropriate in a Catholic college curriculum cost scarcely a fraction of the present (and past and future) outlays for all the paraphernalia that the sciences require.

In short, our education system should be revised to emphasize Catholicity of mind and not the faulty secularism that dominates almost all the non-Catholic colleges.

This is not to say we should abandon these subjects; it is a question of emphasis. If Catholics want to major in these disciplines, then they should go where they can get the best possible education—the secular colleges. There are some, particularly among religious, who dread the thought of young Catholics being exposed to the hazards of secularism, particularly as it might affect their faith. There is validity in this. But just as the youth is trained in the various academic disciplines to prepare him for more advanced study and speculation, so too should his studies in religion and philosophy progress, so that he may achieve intellectual maturity in both. A student in a secular college could continue his religious and philosophical studies under the auspices of his Newman Club, provided these clubs will develop beyond the social centers which most of them now are.

Catholic colleges can never achieve stature in the popular mind, which sees large laboratories, medical centers, engineering schools, football fields, and heavy endowments as the marks of greatness. Let the Catholic campus provide the leaven of Christian culture and ideas. After all, the sciences, particularly those that end in hydrogen bombs, are merely an extension of man's arm. It is the ideas, the thoughts, the philosophies, that fill the mind. And it is the mind that controls the arm.

If this is the ideal, why haven't we achieved it? I suppose for a number of reasons. For so long Catholics in this country, particularly those in the exposed position of education, felt themselves closed in by a hostile society that preferred its Catholics to remain charwomen and entertainers rather than exponents of ideas. Under these difficult circumstances, it was very easy to melt into the academic woodwork and appear intellectually neutral—that is, genuinely American, not pronouncedly Catholic. I don't think economics can be the whipping boy. Ideas cost nothing. For years the American Church has not seen the clash of ideas or developed the intellectuals commensurate with the Catholic population; for years it has been unwilling to experiment forthrightly with new disciplines. The Church in Europe has done this for centuries. We have not even begun to approach it in this regard.

But times have changed. It is clear that other Americans can now accept the idea of Catholic intellectuality, that Rome doesn't dictate fifteenth-century policies to a twentieth-century society. (Especially well received have been Pius XII's views on such subjects as psychotherapy, to say nothing of John XXIII's ecumenical energy which cast a whole new image of the modern Church in the eyes of non-Catholics.)

And yet, despite strong leadership from Europe in general and the popes in particular, American Catholics have made scarcely any impact on the current intellectual and cultural ferment that promises to revolutionize society for centuries to come. Why is this? I believe the primary responsibility lies with Catholic education, especially on the college and university levels, where it is dominated by the Jesuits. The Jesuits, in their position of intellectual authority, have allowed themselves to approach each new academic year with the same defensive attitudes they had the year before. They have not been willing (or perhaps able) to fit new ideas into their centuries-old intellectual discipline and their typically American curriculum. And for a reason, I feel. There are hazards in experimentation, risks in new formulations, dangers in creativity.

For example, psychology is still quite suspect. Some feel that since modern psychology, particularly depth psychology, originated with Freud, whose philosophical meanderings should be no obstacle to an appreciation of his extraordinary discoveries in clinical psychiatry, Catholics simply mustn't have anything to do with the subject. This suspicion and this fear of complicity held Catholic activity back for decades. Even today few Catholic colleges do more than offer a skeleton curriculum in psychology. Sociology, its origins rooted in the materialistic philosophies of the late nineteenth and early twentieth centuries, is similarly suspect, with the result that the Catholic voice is just beginning to be heard.

Further, simply because St. Thomas Aquinas is the official philosopher of the Church, it doesn't follow that nothing has been done since his time. This failure to investigate is reminiscent of the reluctance of public schools to allow courses in communism for fear of its tarnishing Americanism. Only lately has there been a change. A similar change is needed in Catholic colleges regarding alien philosophies.

Literature, incorporating creative writing, has been one of the most neglected subjects in Catholic education. The approach to much of modern writing is almost skittish. There is an appalling aversion to anything sexual, which has brought the wrath of many Catholics—and many non-Catholics—down on Joyce, J. D. Salinger, D. H. Lawrence, Eugene O'Neill, and anyone else whose works contain sexual themes. Catholic educators must stop being so afraid of sex. If the educator thinks that by denying his students access to genuine literature he will preserve their chastity, he need only go to the nearest newsstand and examine the visual and literary pornography that is so readily and inexpensively available. Chastity and purity of mind do not depend on the exclusion of Joyce. On the other hand, the serious student, given true works of literature and provided with literary guidance and moral perspectives, will be far more able to bring Christian values to bear upon the subject than if he is given "safe" but pallid instruction.

What I am really saying, I suspect, is that Catholic educators must acknowledge the existence of the world in which they live. We do not live in a cloister. This is particularly true for the student. To advert again to the analogy of communism courses and their tardy appearance, the Catholic must know, with a profundity that might well be beyond that of most, a great deal of what is going on "out there" in order to cope with it and, it is hoped, do something about it in time. You don't get rid of something by pretending it does not exist, nor do you solve problems when you are ignorant of their nature.

And yet, upon review of the situation of Catholic education on all levels, the really haunting question arises of whether there should be a Catholic education system at all. The opinion is growing that it should be discarded, and that students should receive academic instruction in the public system and religious instruction in some other way, such as through the C.C.D. or a new system yet undiscovered. Basic to this position is the question of the economic survival of the present system. I sometimes feel that this is the only reason some people have for wanting to discard it. We don't seem able to knock down the "wall of separation," nor can we get federal aid. In other words, we have to go it alone—a just outcome, really, since we created the system. Now we want to be bailed out; but I'm afraid we've made our bed and will have to lie in it, unless we drop the whole thing.

Of course, we could take a hint from the Negroes (who are developing remarkable techniques for getting things done), and threaten the public system with the immediate enrollment of *all* Catholic students. This would produce an unbearable strain on the public schools which we could then relieve by generously offering to keep our system if the government will give it just a bit of subsidy. Then, money in hand, we could threaten some more for more money. We could conceivably do that—we are subtly doing it now—but that is not exactly honorable. It's like a man voluntarily incurring a debt and then threatening not to pay unless the debt is reduced. If we kept it up the debt could be erased—and the Catholic system could be largely subsidized by non-Catholics. Rather a neat trick. But it doesn't solve the question, which is not actually so much economic as philosophical.

The really fundamental question is this: do we need a Catholic education system in America today or in the future? If not, let's drop it—sell all the land and buildings, invest the proceeds in mutual funds—and use the public schools. On the other hand, if a special system is really necessary, then we must transform a faulty system into one of true value, one that will warrant the enormous economic outlay we are currently making and the even greater sacrifices lying ahead.

To arrive at an answer, we must view not only the situation and needs of the Catholic, but also his setting in modern society.

The most important thing in a Catholic's life is his faith. Without it life would have no meaning, death being nothing more than an ending. To the Catholic, death is just a beginning; all that goes before is a prelude, a preparation. But the Catholic doesn't live in a sanctuary counting his beads; while he is not of this world, he is in it. Actually, he is in it as a missionary to all mankind, not only to the distant and exotic pagans but more frequently and directly to his neighbors. Beyond this, he lives a temporal life in which he must support himself and his family, finding a station—a vocation—that will involve him in a great variety of temporal concerns. It must be remembered, though, that foremost is his concern for the eternal; all that is temporal is intended to lead him and all mankind to the eternal. So, in a special sense, everything he learns, everything he does, has great eschatological significance, and without this significance temporal life would be pointless.

Education is not an isolated temporal activity without teleological significance, but is bound to it. To compartmentalize man into an educational being and a religious being would contradict the fact that all truth is one; to attempt to divorce learning from truth would destroy meaning itself. How ancient is Pilate's question, "What is truth?" And how obvious was the answer standing before him! Yet the modern world repeats the same question with the same disordered answer: "There is no such thing as truth." This grotesque theory holds that we may search for truth, but we will never find it. This is not only nonsensical; it leads to total futility, even madness. It is like searching for a needle in the haystack when no needle is there in the first place.

But the Catholic maintains that truth can be arrived at. *This* is what marks him off from the relativist, who wanders in ever-decreasing circles; *this* is the Catholic's great gift. And it is so intimately intertwined with his religious views that they cannot be separated. As a result, religion and education cannot be divorced; however, a shift of orientation is needed.

Probably the one word that best describes the modern age is *secular*. Outside a few communities like the Catholic, some Protestant, and Jewish, the contention is that God doesn't exist, or if He does, He doesn't have anything to do with us. America today is particularly prone to this aberration. Especially divested of spirituality is the education structure, which has seen a constant dwindling away of inherited religious attitudes and practices. Modern American education is almost totally secular; shortly it will be absolutely so. All we need are a few more Supreme Court decisions.

The only major force conflicting with secularism in modern American education is the Catholic Church with its education system. Do away with this force and in one generation the national community, not just the education sector, would be secular. Without the redeeming factor of the Catholic perspective, America would be taking its final drift down into spiritual suicide.

So there is no question of dropping the Catholic education system. But it *must* be transformed into something far greater and more potent than it is today. Otherwise, we will stumble along, generally preserving the faith but otherwise having very little to offer, not only to Catholics but also to the rest of American society.

What best describes the Catholic system is its general air of piety. What least characterizes it is its scholarship. This arises out of the fact that the system is religion-orientated and not education-orientated, and is, furthermore, run by nonprofessionals. This is a criticism, of course, and yet we must recognize in all fairness that historical necessity has brought us to the present point of difficulty. Historically, the Church chose to set up a separate system for religious reasons, and at its inception there were few besides priests and nuns capable of running the schools.

But times have changed in two significant ways: first, the laity have grown in quality as well as quantity; second, priests and religious are in constantly greater demand to perform their primary duties. The population grows, but the priests and religious are not growing in proportion. Out of these two facts arises an obvious solution, both for pragmatic reasons and, more importantly, in philosophical terms.

The laity should take charge of the Catholic education system, not merely extending their participation as subordinate teachers but also administering it from top to bottom. I realize this may sound like rank heresy to traditionalists, particularly those who have a vested interest in not rocking the boat. But before everyone shouts "Anathema!" let's take an honest look at the suggestion.

To begin with, it must be remembered that the system would still be under the jurisdiction of the local bishops, who have had in the past and would have in the future the authority to control, regulate, and change personnel and policies. It is irksome to have to begin this way, but bishops have an inbred tendency to assume that whenever a layman suggests active participation in the affairs of the Church, he is trying to take over. Such is not the case; we merely want to serve the Church as constituent, not associate, members. It is probably necessary to repeat again that the layman is just as much a part of the Church as a bishop. It is precisely because the layman *is* part of the Mystical Body that he can do the job. In fact, he can do the job better than anyone else.

The bishops, so long immersed in the corporate structure, really don't know too much about the rest of the Church or secular society; here is where the layman has an advantage. He is not only a member of the Church but also a member of secular society.

Authority and responsibility are not alien to the layman's experience, which bishops don't seem too aware of. It is true, nevertheless; the layman learns to accept authority from obedience in childhood and adolescence, obedience in his professional life, and obedience to the bishop's authority. But he also practices authority—over his children, over subordinates in business, in civic affairs. And then, too, there is the odd suspicion that a bishop may lack confidence in his own powers of appointment. How does he know that the cleric he appoints to head the diocesan system is really qualified? Did five handy priests draw straws? Of course not. No bishop would appoint an obviously inadequate superintendent of schools. He bases his choice on the man's experience, his record, and the special qualities needed for the particular office. Could not a layman be so qualified?

Yet laymen are not considered for these tasks, as we know. Bishops appoint employees of the corporate structure for two reasons: internal discipline, and the fact that the appointee is a member of the Church. Bishops just don't want outsiders running things. And laymen are outsiders. The flaw in this outlook is twofold: first, that discipline is internal, and second, that the layman is an outsider.

No university president is a power by himself. He neither

owns nor controls; he runs. Over every president there is a board of trustees or, in a state school, the governor. Always there is control; but the wiser the selection, the less control is exercised. This rests on the wisdom of the board, the governor, or the bishop.

The second flaw is to think of the layman as an outsider. He is not. True, he may not be an employee of the corporate structure (and this is the rub), but he is most decidedly a member of the Church. And yet, if bishops could accept the idea of a layman's heading the diocesan school system, he would then be an employee—assuming we must argue so foolishly. However, the concept of lay participation is not founded on the layman's formal desire to be a part of the corporate structure, but rather on the general recognition of his ability to bring something unique and enhancing to the field of Catholic education. And in this regard, I will not use the term *layman* but rather the word *teacher* to define the vocation properly.

The teacher, when he is Catholic, is an intimate of both the secular and the Catholic world. What distinguishes him decisively is his vocation as a teacher—but not a teacher in the popular American sense. He is not a secularist; he is a Catholic whose vocation is teaching. Again, he teaches to impart not factual knowledge only but knowledge in its universal sense of incorporating the temporal into the eternal. He incorporates into one being the temporal and the eternal. Added to this is the concept of vocation.

The argument may be raised that many laymen are already in the system. This is true, but the layman presently in the system is in a distinctly subservient and indeed intolerable position. On all levels of education and in all cases, the layman is junior to and subject to the cleric or religious. We in America pride ourselves on the fact that someone born in a log cabin can become President, that today's stockboy can become tomorrow's corporation executive, that a sodajerk can become a great movie star, that the janitor's son can become the captain of the school's football team. We Americans have many dreams, but one we can never have: a layman's becoming head of a diocesan school system. He may offer his services and talents, but he can only go so far.

Beyond this is the well-known fact that on a campus where there are both clerical and lay faculty members, the layman occupies an inferior status. He is a second-class citizen. He may have all the ability in the world, but on each campus there is always the feeling that he is present both at the sufferance of the clerics and because there is a shortage of help; he is considered a substitute teacher. He is made acutely aware of the fact that if there were enough clerics to go around he wouldn't even have a job. This attitude is unendurable, whether we talk of elementary, secondary, or college teaching. There is, it is true, the polite charade of lay faculty organizations, committees, and even "senates," but they are a mockery; let a layman press a point and his contract is simply not renewed. But more onerous than technicalities are the subtleties that discolor the relationships on a Catholic campus. Probably the best way to describe them is to refer to the relationship that exists between the clergy and the laity. The key to it all is the feeling on the part of the clergy that they have *arrived,* while the layman is hopelessly lost in his efforts to become something more than he is.

In any discussion such as this there is the very obvious rejoinder: if you don't like it, forget it and go somewhere else. This, of course, is very true; the layman can say with varying degrees of annoyance, "The hell with the lot of you," but it would in no way solve the problem. What every bishop and every priest must realize is that a tremendous number of laymen, as members of the Mystical Body of Christ, care enough about the Church to want to give their lives to its service. Just because God calls us to different vocations within the Church doesn't mean that those of us not called to the sacramental life love the Church less. What we are saying is that we have something unique and worthy to give to the Church, and here I am talking of the layman's great gift of his vocation as a teacher.

To be a teacher, however, involves more than being a secondary sort of person; it means the opportunity, given the talents and predisposition, to advance, not remain forever subject to and beneath another on the basis simply of arbitrary power. There is nothing inherent in being a layman that forbids development and authority. And until the authorities realize this, they will continue to discourage lay participation—equal participation—in Catholic education.

Naturally, I am not suggesting segregation, with laymen in the system and others outside it. This would be to deny the inalienable rights of the priest and religious. It would be very like the situation of keeping Negroes out of white schools. No, this is not the idea. Rather than exclude priests and religious, we should have proper integration of the education system. Just as the federal government is trying to create parity in its various departments, the Catholic education system should endeavor to do the same. No one should be denied advancement because the color of his vocation is different. Advancement should be based on merit, which is not the case now. The result is that many qualified men and women refuse to enter the system because it blatantly discriminates against them.

And yet there are many lay people in the system who have sacrificed other careers for that of serving the Church. Unfortunately, many drift out again, not only because they can't advance beyond a certain point but also because of the stigma that is attached to being a layman.

Beyond these points, there is a further basis for lay parity in education. We see such a vocation as naturally belonging to the laity. We see, further, the terrible need for priests and religious to fulfill their primary vocations, not in the center of the Catholic ghetto but on the frontiers of society.

Just recently I had occasion to visit a Catholic college campus when, with the ringing of the noon bell, scores of nuns converged on the dining room. It was a lovely day, just outside of San Francisco among the gentle hills, and everything was very pleasant. For a moment I was overwhelmed by the sight of so many religious concentrated in one spot. Then I realized that it was wrong: they shouldn't be there, so closely congregated. I thought of all those others, in California, the rest of America, the world, who had no one to care for them, to nurse them, to teach them, to bring them the sacraments.

Priests and religious are the settlers of the world's frontiers; no one else can really take their place. Having left family and friends, they offer themselves to Christ. Only, their superiors send them to teach and nurse too close to Rome. Always we hear the cry that there is a shortage of vocations, and yet how many who take the vows wander outside the safe confines of the Christian camp? How many novices prayed for a chance to serve the poor, the sick, the ignorant, and instead were sent to coach subdebs in the niceties of French literature? True, the Church needs its saints everywhere, but must so many in so few places serve so few?

We are all members of the Mystical Body, each of us with his abilities; and everywhere there is need for our various faculties and talents. Just as the laity should never bury their talents, neither should the priests and religious squander theirs. The ideal is for each to occupy a proper niche in the Church. Some are ordained to carry the sacraments to the ends of the earth, and some to go where others fear to go, to feed, to clothe, to teach; others have the more constrained opportunity to fill the void left by those who find themselves on the frontiers of society. This is an ancient thing, this Church of ours, and it can only renew itself in sacrifice, not in gentle decline or in polishing silver at a young lady's finishing school.

7 ❧

ART AND ARTIFICE

THE major difficulty in trying to discuss the arts with Catholics, both lay and religious, is the disconcerting fact that the majority of one's audience haven't the slightest idea of what it's all about. Mention art and then stare into blank faces—that is what one must expect.

Art was once a rather casual, even intimate, part of the lives of those who rejoiced in being considered Catholic. The Church, in all its worldliness, was the major patron of the arts. Indeed, it is hard to tell who was more eager—the artists to draw near the Chair of St. Peter, or the Chair to inch closer and closer to the fashionable artists. Inevitably, in any discussion of the Church and art, one's attention is directed to the magnificent works of Fra Angelico, Botticelli, Da Vinci, and particularly Michelangelo and Bernini, who were so largely responsible for the Basilica of St. Peter. It is a source of parochial pride to realize that so many of the great masters glorified the Catholic Church; only in later ages did artists tend to leave the Church to its own dcvices and go about portraying common men doing very ordinary things, such as sitting for a family portrait or drifting down a stream.

There was actually a period in history when the Church respected the arts, encouraged them, and saw to it that they had a place of dignity among the professions. Of course, this was in an age when the Church—or rather, the bishops —had an eye for beauty. Further, they weren't ashamed of their own tastes. True, there were bishops who insisted on fig leaves and strategic wisps of hair, and there were bishops who put a number of works away from the public's untutored gaze (usually hiding them in their private residences), and a few manuscripts were consigned to obscure shelves of libraries; but still there was enormous respect for the arts. Painting, sculpture, architecture, literature, music were part and parcel of Christian life. The arts, in their mysterious way, translated the revealed into the understood, the suspected into the realized, the hidden into the obvious. But then, that was an age of faith.

In the Age of Enlightenment, when the Christian churches went on the defensive, and puritanism was the rising ethic, the arts became suspected of the most terrible mischief. No one could stand before the blatant carnality of the human form without the necessary blushes appropriate to his faith. No mind could wallow in the intellectual licentiousness of the emerging novelist or poet without exposing his latent heresy. Music, once so safely Gregorian, broke in upon spiritual decorum with its lascivious harmonies, certain to corrupt the choir of the young. There was something presumptuous about art: it dared to exist independent of the bishops.

Whereas once art could stand naked and unadorned as something good in and of itself, in time, under the pressure of the Protestant Reformation and the emergence of the moralistic middle class, art came to be viewed either as the work of the devil or else as work which had to serve a more noble purpose than giving aesthetic pleasure; it had to serve the purposes of the various bishops. That is, art should exist for the Church, with the aim of edifying and otherwise indoctrinating. So to prostitute genius, so to cripple one of man's most glorious activities is to pervert it, much as it would be a perversion of nature to require every rose to form a soft-petaled cross—and not merely a cross, if some clerics had their way, but a cross bearing a steadily bleeding corpus, over the head of which other petals would describe in perfect script the eternal letters INRI.

It need hardly be pointed out that one of the worst collective offenders against artistic taste has been the Catholic Church in America. America, it must be confessed, is terribly blessed with mediocrity, in terms not only of Church-oriented art but of art generally. There are, of course, two basic factors which account for the paucity of any genuine Catholic art in this country.

To begin with, we have the hostile heritage of Puritanism, which viewed any artistic adornment as the work of Lucifer—not metaphorically but quite literally. We are a plain folk, without any sauce, who have hewed an empire out of the wilderness. This makes us particularly rugged, with coarse hands and strong backs. We know the truth about artists: they are womanish, decadent—sissies, if you will. And all in the service of Lucifer who seeks to seduce our plain folk away from their duty of chopping down trees and planting corn in the south forty.

Second, Catholics, ever anxious to be part of the national family, severed all aesthetic ties with European Catholicism and, if possible, became more puritan than the Puritans who engulfed New England. Actually, in all things, Catholics have made pathetic attempts to be *liked* by the rest of society.

Inherent in the problem of the American Church and art is the role played by the Irish. If one peculiarity marks the Church in this country, it is the dominance by the Irish. However, the Irish to whom I allude are not the leprechaun-loving and dancing-of-the-jig sort of Irish, but rather those Irish clerics who have historically ruled Ireland with a mailed fist. While Ireland has produced its share of amusement, it has also produced a type of Churchman who has almost stifled freedom. Naturally, he can offer all sorts of rationalizations—they come so easily to support repression—for why the Irish Church, through its devoted servants, the clergy, must sit on society to the point of suffocation. But the fact remains that the Church in Ireland has been and still is infamous for its authoritarian regulation of every phase of Irish life, and particularly for the suppression of artistic efforts. One doesn't have to suggest Joyce; one can refer to the problems of such internationally recognized masters as Synge, O'Connor, and O'Casey to lay bare the nonsense of hierarchical censorship.

This repressive, ignorant, Philistine segment of the

Church merely transplanted itself into American soil in the nineteenth century. The result is a clergy in America overwhelmed by the Irish, who have brought with them their ancient prejudice against anything they don't understand.

This really is the problem. Not only do we have to contend with the Irish clerical disposition; we are also faced with the clergy's general ignorance about art. It could hardly be otherwise. Coming here, as so many did, a century ago, the Irish brought with them little more than body and soul, plus a serious need to feed the body and protect the soul on alien shores. There was little time for niceties; a man had to work to support his family. No nonsense in this sort of life. All this is quite legitimate, but one can't lose sight of the fact that these people were Irish as well as poor. The curse has not left the American scene. True, there are a few priests and bishops who can raise their sights above a good and sensible diet, but the great majority simply can't see the difference between art and artifice. What serves to decorate the Church is tolerable as long as it is the sort of thing one experienced in Ireland. All else is the work of the devil—that is, they don't understand it.

We have the Irish; what fun to conjecture about what it would be like if the French or Italian or Spanish dominated the American Church! Three great artistic civilizations have lost out to the Irish, whose only significant contribution has been to supply us with St. Patrick's Day parades and shillelaghs! But it would be unfair to place all the blame on Irish Philistinism; in all probability, the massive Anglo-Saxon influence in America would have seriously handicapped any efforts at real art—that is, until sometime around the First World War.

While America produced very little worthwhile art of any sort during the eighteenth and nineteenth centuries, it began a sort of barbaric renaissance some fifty years ago. Critics argued over Dreiser, Hemingway, Dos Passos, Fitzgerald, and others, but this was far better than the Catholic silence that was yet to be broken by anyone of universally recognized talent.

The really basic question in art concerns its function. Should art be an end in itself or should it be a means to an end? To the Christian the answer seems quite simple: art is a means. In opposition to the view of the Christian (and all those who are religiously oriented) is the principle of art for art's sake, an attitude that refuses to place art in any context other than a vague one called "aesthetics." Morality, particularly Christian morality, can play no part. While at first blush this may seem anti-Christian, it really isn't. What this school is protesting against is the false figure of Christianity that has overshadowed Western civilization for perhaps the last three hundred years.

This misunderstanding is very like the confusion over Freud and his contention that all religions are nothing more than a particular expression of neurosis. A further examination of his views, considered in their proper context—late nineteenth-century Vienna—makes it quite clear that Freud knew nothing about real Christianity. He was acquainted only with the corrupt practices and institutions of a thoroughly dispirited society. It was against these that he constructed his principle, which, when properly understood, makes a great deal of sense. It is completely accurate to say that such a religious state *was* a form of neurosis—a neurosis born of the trauma experienced at the time of the Protestant Reformation and fed by the neurotic concepts of Reason and Enlightenment.

No artist works in a vacuum, and despite constant protestations from all sides, the artist impresses on his work a certain philosophy, whether implied or expressed, unconscious or conscious. However, sometimes it takes probing to find. Of course, the philosophy that informs a work of art may not be particularly sophisticated or very beneficial; but it is nevertheless present, even where it is manifestly absent, even if all the artist's work seems to say are such things as "There is no God, no purpose to life, no hope," or "God is a miserable bastard because I'm a miserable bastard," or "Zen—isn't it the greatest?" or "Nothing, nothing, nothing."

The point is that all art fits into a philosophical or moral context, whether the artist will admit it or not. And it is also true that this context may change from work to work. Monday the artist may love life, and Tuesday may find him suffering from the flu and overdue bills. The truth is that there is no such thing as "art for art's sake."

There then remains the alternative: art is a means to an end. And it is because art is a means to an end that the Catholic Church in America has seized on it as a splendid means to convert the world to Catholicism, as well as a sop to the aesthetic needs of Catholics. Only, the Church has failed miserably on both counts.

Actually, art isn't any one thing; it is a fusing of several

things. The key to understanding the nature of art—which
is prerequisite to understanding its function—is the concept
of aesthetics or aesthetic experience.

A work of art is an artificial creation. It may be a particular arrangement of colors, forms, words, sounds, tex-
tures, movements. Take an oil painting. It is a piece of
ordinary canvas, a flat surface, on which are placed various
colors squeezed out of tubes and applied to the canvas by
brush, fingers, or anything else available. When the artist
has completed his painting and we view it, we see none of
that; we see a landscape or a beautiful woman.

And yet, to say "we see a landscape or a beautiful
woman" is utter nonsense—that is, unless we suspend normal logic and objectivity. True, we view the art work with
part of our minds; otherwise we would not recognize the
landscape. But more: somehow we react to what is before
us. This moment, then, becomes an emotional experience,
but an emotional experience tempered by the intellect. It is
this fusing of our several faculties that is the aesthetic experience.

In order for this aesthetic experience to occur, there is
always the necessity of a proper balance between intellect
and emotion. This is the artist's burden. If he becomes didactic or too cerebral, his work will diminish as art; it will
be more a dissertation or formal equation. On the other
hand, emotion alone will result in chaos; there is a vast
difference between a shout and a controlled high C. The
power in the act of creation is the emotional energy of the
artist, diffused and undirected. The intellect, ordered and

directed, works to give form to this formless effusion. Both are necessary to creation.

But art is more than this. And so is the aesthetic experience. Why is it that we see a landscape, hear a symphony, read a poem? Why should a bunch of colors, sounds, or symbols produce a remarkable effect on us when all they are is a bunch of colors, sounds, or symbols?

Man does not live by bread alone; neither does he find fulfillment in merely preparing that bread. If life moved on such a level, it would prove the materialistic fallacy. Man is also a spiritual being, touched by the unseen and moved by the unspoken. It is because of man's restless dissatisfaction with the apparent world that he seeks to discover another. Since he cannot escape his time and place, man wonders, and out of this wonder he creates his own visions, his own dreams, which find their way onto canvas and paper. The landscape isn't really the actual landscape seen by the natural eye; it is transformed in order to lay bare the essences *behind* the obvious. To express oneself in artistic forms is to search, to find, and to reveal the spiritual. This is what drives the artist; and it is this that moves the viewer. Every work of art contains within it some small particle of the eternal—the eternal corrupt, perfect, confused, hated, loved, feared, but always the eternal as felt by the artist and as seen by the viewer.

What makes art of *Oedipus Rex,* Michelangelo's *Moses,* Beethoven's *Ninth Symphony? War and Peace, The Divine Comedy, Hamlet?* Can mere words, marble, sounds, or patterned movements conspire to overwhelm man if they are just that and no more? What makes them art is the lifting, ever so slightly, of the veil of mystery that man seeks to penetrate, the mystery that is eternity. Man yearns for something ineffable, and art, for a moment at least, satisfies that yearning by helping him glimpse that something which gives life meaning. How terrible to be just a maker of bread! How empty the grave if it were the final answer!

The mind may try to prove the existence of God and eternal life, but only the heart can convince us that it is all really true. Again, we have the intellect and the emotions—the fusion producing the aesthetic experience which helps us grasp what man might become, not only now but forever. No mere rhetoric is Hamlet's cry, "The play's the thing wherein I'll catch the conscience of the King!"

It is strange that out of something artificial, the work of art, can emerge a reality that is far beyond our ability to grasp fully. Again and again we return to a painting or a symphony or any other work that has once caught the inner eye or ear. Each time we revisit the provocative moment of experience we discover something previously hidden. It is as if we grow in wisdom, without actually knowing how or why.

Art, then, is no toy or diversion. But art is cursed with a danger that threatens to destroy not only the artist but art itself, and this because it involves the act of creation, which is no toy or diversion either.

The greatest danger facing the artist is pride—pride that can threaten him with the megalomaniacal fantasy that he is God. Humility in the presence of personal power is the desideratum, but it is too often lacking. As a consequence, the art may survive but the artist may perish. However, pride can even corrupt the works themselves if the artist bends them more and more to his own will and refuses them a life of their own. This occurs when the artist loses his naturalness and produces self-conscious works that serve to enhance the artist and not to express the art. When this happens, art gives way to artifice.

Viewed more broadly, the danger attending art is the danger that attends all creation; that is, what has been created? It is one thing to gaze rapturously at the ceiling of the Sistine Chapel and an entirely different thing to come across the writings of the Marquis de Sade. The Christian reacts one way to *The Diary of a Country Priest* and rather differently to *Candide*. History is filled with examples of art that horrify and degrade as well as exalt. The obvious question arises: should art be censored? And if so, who is going to do it?

But these questions put the cart before the horse. Personally, I would like to get rid of all art that offends my personal taste. There are many church buildings, pious paintings, and unctuous writings I would love to do away with, just as I would like to keep profane art that is morally repugnant out of my path. Actually, there appear to be two bases for decision: bad art and bad morals. Should we just protect morals or should we also do away with what we consider aesthetically bad? At this point we should do neither. We should first ask this question: does the artist have a right to produce whatever he wants? Certainly. To say otherwise is to deny him freedom.

I have intentionally reversed the order of the two considerations—censorship and the right to produce—in order to expose the flaw in most Catholic thinking. Because most Catholics don't understand art, all they can think and talk about is censorship. Based on ignorance, censorship not only keeps from the public what it censors but also scares artists away from natural expression and substitutes for it self-conscious artifice, designed not as an art work but as a means of getting past the censors. This is an utter perversion of art. And it helps explain why very few Catholic Americans warrant the title of artist.

Reversing the usual process, what about the artist and his art? First of all, we cannot discuss the artist as a man; that is his private affair. What concerns us is the relationship of the work of art to society.

If man is really free, subject only to conscience, then the artist should—indeed, *must*—be free to create as he will, with absolutely no regard to society or censorship. Creativity must be unself-conscious in order to produce an authentic art work. The artist, when functioning as an artist, has as his highest responsibility his total dedication to his work. He must be true to it and it alone, out of love for what he creates. Anything less would be a betrayal of himself as an artist and of his work. He has no right to defraud what he creates of its completion to the best of his ability.

Once the act of creation has been completed, the artist, in a sense, passes away and the critic takes over. The critic (censor, if you will) is the man who the moment before was the artist. Every artist must criticize his work in order to determine whether or not it deserves the name *art* and whether or not this art should be presented to others. This is not unlike the procedure one applies to a thought that enters the mind, whether bidden or unbidden. Should the thought be uttered, or is silence better? Notice, however, that there is no contention that the thought should not be allowed into the mind. Sometimes attempts are made to do this; these attempts are classified clinically as either suppression or repression and are an integral part of neurosis and psychosis.

The question now confronting the artist-turned-critic is one of discretion, and it goes to the heart of the matter: what is the basis of artistic criticism?

The basis is comparison. For there to be a critical consideration of a particular work, there must be some sort of standard with which it can be matched.

Or, put another way, the particular work must be compared with other generally comparable work.

The error of those who proclaim art for art's sake, like that of Catholic (or Christian) would-be critics, is that they each have only one standard. The former look only to the organic standard, while the latter observe only the dynamic. The fault of each school lies in its failure to observe the other's standard as well as its own. Catholics tend to relate all art to God, concluding that a "bad" poem about God is better than a "good" poem about something else. Their opposite numbers seem to say, "We don't care what you say as long as you say it well." Both groups are guilty of faulty judgment.

Proper criticism rests on both the organic and the dynamic principle; each alone is worthless. Essentially, the two principles ask two prime questions: what is it, and how does it fit into the scheme of things?

Organic analysis takes the work and, without regard to its place in any particular scheme, determines whatever apparent merit the work possesses in terms of craft. Essentially, this raises two more questions: what is the artist attempting, and how well does he do it? A tendency among Catholic critics is to refuse to probe into what the artist is attempting if they suspect for a moment that something is dynamically wrong. For example, a particular work by a certain author with a reputation for writing along certain lines simply won't get a fair reading; the critics will not even *see* the work supposedly under study, but only other, earlier works. They prejudge the present on the basis of the past.

The first point, therefore, is to see what the artist is attempting. Then the critic must determine how well the artist has done in this particular instance. This requires training and experience as well as taste. A theater critic should know the theater—its history, its conventions, its various forms, the long line of writers who have written for the stage. Needless to say, for the time he must completely suspend dynamic analysis, which has no business cropping up until the organic merits of the work have been thoroughly explored.

This requires fair play for those with whom we disagree as well as for those who have our warmest sympathies, a principle Catholic critics are prone to ignore in their enthusiasm to support a Catholic artist and their equal enthusiasm to denigrate most others, particularly those clearly at odds with Catholic principles. Charity should enter at such

a point, but it seldom does, except as the thin garb of senti-
mentality or cold scrutiny. It is not at all easy to make a fair
organic analysis of writers like Voltaire or Zola when one
thoroughly opposes their views, but if the critic can't keep
his opinions under control through this phase, he has no
business being a critic. He is as useful as a surgeon who
can't stand the sight of blood.

Generally, organic analysis will tend to distinguish the
genius from the also-ran. In terms of great gifts, it really
doesn't matter whether we agree or not; we recognize the
talent for what it is. This we can admire. It is a basic fact of
my own critical life that I dislike the philosophical perspective of Tennessee Williams, but I must admire his drama-
turgical talent. On the other hand, we have Morris L. West,
obviously well-intentioned but an abysmally bad writer.
Poulenc's philosophical tendencies caused a great deal of
concern, nevertheless he wrote profoundly spiritual music
such as, *Les Dialogues des Carmelites*. Edward Stone's
talent is apparent whether he designs an embassy or a
hospital. And there is even great merit in a well-conceived
and well-executed television commercial, whether we care
for the particular product or not. All this admiration (or
the opposite) is derived from an awareness of the task the
artist set himself and how well he did his work.

This sort of criticism is not inherently difficult if one
brings a certain technical and aesthetic facility to his task.
The challenge of complete criticism comes in the next step,
that of analyzing the dynamics of the work. Here we must
ask ourselves how the particular work fits into the scheme
of things. Immediately there arises the further question:

what is meant by "the scheme of things?" It can best be answered by posing the preliminary question, where is it going? Or put another way, where is the artist trying to lead *us?* We may climb into a Cadillac, but our destination is actually determined by whether the Cadillac is a hearse or a convertible.

Every artist is really a master in the art of seduction. He attempts to move us in some direction or other, not through our minds alone (which never works) but through our emotions given form by the artist's intellectual and often hidden intention. If someone is convinced that determinism governs man's actions, he presents this intellectual conviction in such a way as to convert others to this belief. All artists, all thinkers, seek converts to their beliefs. The philosopher presents his case one way, the politician another, and the writer still another. Some may object that this is a rather cynical view of art, but what if I were to replace the principle of determinism with the principle of free will, or with the Christian principle of redemptive suffering?

The point is that the artist feels something very deeply; if he didn't he would probably be a businessman or a plumber. The artist has a vision which he must communicate to others. This marks him off from all others, who may have visions or feel deeply but who are not at all driven to communicate to the world. This is not to say one is better than the other; they merely have different ways of life.

The essential task of dynamic analysis is to determine the latent content of the work as distinct from the manifest content. The obvious analogy is with a dream, in which the really significant thing is not the manifest content but the latent content; when this is uncovered it truly reveals what is happening in the unconscious of the dreamer. The same thing holds true of the artist. What is the artist really saying? And what does he want of us?

Once we answer these questions, particularly the latter, we then must ask ourselves the final question: do we, too, want this for ourselves? To arrive at an answer we must know first where we are, dynamically speaking, and then where we want to go independently of the artist. Seduction is not in itself a bad thing—or good, for that matter. A man may well seduce his wife, but certainly not the wife of another.

So it is with the artist. And this requires the critic to bring to his work a viable philosophy of life. It cannot be a dimly felt thing or a weak hypothesis subject to every current and eddy of thought. The critic must know just as thoroughly what he stands for as what the artist stands for. The absence of either destroys his value as a critic.

There really isn't much of a problem when critic and artist are two of a kind and are headed for the same goals, but what about the situation where the critic stands for one thing and the artist for another? This is a particularly thorny problem for a Christian critic analyzing the work of an anti-Christian, and it has confounded Catholic critics who are far more Catholic than critical.

If this were a perfect society it is unlikely that we would have artists; the ideal and the real would be one, and there would be no tension through divorce, nothing hidden yet yearned for. We would be one vast family swimming in common agreement and merely marking time until we

move ahead to well-deserved rewards. But this is not the
way things are. We are in a terribly imperfect world,
molded largely by sin and subject to the most invidious
vices. Out of this imperfection it is only reasonable to an-
ticipate a generous flow of contradiction and debate. Man
suffers and cries out; quite often it is the artist's cry that is
most forcibly impressed on the universal conscience. We
rather appreciate his cry when it happens that we concur;
we take a dim view of his caterwauling when he travels
another course. It is very easy to assume ourselves to be
blessed with insight and correctness (it is such a Godlike
quality) and everyone else to be steeped in malevolent error. It is another thing to pause and question ourselves as
well as grant, at the very least, some decent intentions to
another. Easiest of all is to thumb through the *Baltimore
Catechism* or St. Thomas for all of life's answers. This is, of
course, the usual method in much Catholic criticism.

Let us take but one glaring example: Voltaire. He was a
nasty man who preached all sorts of immoral ideas and
publicly ridiculed the Church. Such an anti-Christian deserved short shrift if not actual excommunication. But is
this entirely so? Rather than satisfy ourselves with a horrified glimpse at his work, it might be well for us to place
Voltaire in his historical setting, eighteenth-century France,
whose so-called Catholicism (to say nothing of Christianity) is one of the great scandals of history. Without question, the Church that existed in France at that time was
corrupt and as anti-Christian in spirit as any Church could
possibly be. Such being the case, Voltaire was probably far

more Christian than the harlots he attacked. Yet Voltaire was a nasty man.

Much the same sort of argument can be raised today. The artists of our time are largely rebelling against their society. This is just as obvious in the abstract painter and the mechanic struggling to formulate electronic music as it is in the great bulk of our present writers. Those of us who are convinced we have the answers should reflect upon—and respect—those who are just slightly less optimistic and assured. Further, we might just possibly set about changing the things that contradict our conceited theories. We may profess the brotherhood of man, but do we practice it? Not for a moment. We talk endlessly about love of God, but do we actually go beyond pious phrases? Not for a moment. We insist on the sanctity of life, but do we grant life a shred of dignity? Not for a moment. You and I may be perfect, sir, but our actions are abominable.

The truth is that the artist sees the evils of the world and seeks some tentative reconciliation between what is and what should be. For one reason or another, he may suggest solutions incompatible with our thinking, but still he deserves our serious attention because he is really commenting on *us*. Therefore, when the artist speaks, rather than look up appropriate passages in the catechism we should peer honestly into the mirror of our conscience. We may not like what the artist presents, but after all, he is only revealing us to ourselves. Rather than try to convert the artist, we should begin to think about converting ourselves. It is not the artist who lies; it is we, who are the nasty men

of our times. We manage to fool everyone—everyone, that
is, except the artist.

All of this has to do with art, not artifice, which
scarcely deserves the dignity of being linked with art, and
wouldn't be if so much of our critical time weren't taken up
with artifice. Furthermore, our creative faculties are also
perversely focused on the trivia of artifice. The results are
the precarious health of art and the bloat of pap.

To many Catholics art exists for only one purpose: to
prove that the Church of Rome, and only the Church of
Rome, is the one true Church, and that all those obstinately
resisting its maternal admonitions are running an almost
certain risk of not only temporal loss but eternal as well.
There is rather a grain of truth in the Church's assertion,
but I prefer the thought that art's ultimate function is to
bring men to God. It is one thing to rely on God's grace,
but entirely another to rely on the bad taste of some Irish-
man whose only brush with art was a daily walk in the
seminary between rows of commercial likenesses of dead
bishops.

The creative act can produce all sorts of things that
one can't predict with certainty. Far better to set those
voluptuaries aside and get that pious house servant who
won't cause any trouble. Besides, the act of creation is an
act of pride, and everyone knows that only the humble will
be saved. The truth is that art cannot exist; it must serve.

A thing of beauty, whether it is a couplet or a rose,
deserves to be because it is a reflection of God's beauty.
And this is true whether it appears to serve the Church of
Rome or not.

That fact requires each of us to resist the temptation to clutch at the beautiful thing as if to keep it for ourselves alone. Beauty is to be shared just as God's love is to be shared. Finally, one must not be embarrassed by the presence of beauty. Beauty is not unmanly. Rather, it is virile, coursing with life. An impotent never sires.

What I have said is not intended to impugn the integrity of the American clergy. History has worked against them, first, because many of them come from a repressive and fearful culture that has constrained and stifled all the human creative instincts; and second, because this country, from farm to factory, is more intent on producing men of grit than men of sensitivity. Everyone knows who such men as the Four Horsemen and the Galloping Ghost are, without even needing to hear their real names. How many have heard of Allen Tate or Albert Camus, or even the Bard of Avon?

The average priest can give a detailed rundown on the Series, but has he so much as visited an art gallery? He follows the national political conventions with the instincts of a politician, but does he know either what the Pulitzer Prizes are or who won the most recent ones? He can throw a ball behind the rectory, but does he ever listen to a symphony? He watches "Gunsmoke," but has he ever read Dostoevsky? or Faulkner? He reads the sport page, but has he ever read Aristotle's *Poetics?* Has he ever done anything besides be a priest? Never. And yet this totally untrained, unsympathetic, unaware man has set the course of Catholic participation in the arts for centuries.

Simply because a man happens to be a priest doesn't

give him license to lift up ugly monuments that reflect his appalling aesthetic ignorance. Ordination does not confer critical faculties, despite the baleful efforts of ill-read priests to prescribe what is popularly described as "wholesome" art. And yet, because we are so overwhelmed by the clergy, we take them for our masters even where they have no qualifications whatsoever. This is based on the age-old principle that "Father knows best," or rather, "Father knows," with the obvious corollary that others *don't* know.

Naturally, one might argue, if such is the case, why not allow the clergy to go their way in such matters while the rest of us decide things for ourselves? A marvelous suggestion, except for the annoying fact that art and criticism, in the eyes of the clergy, are not disciplines in themselves, but are merely departments of morality, religion, and inevitably, discipline. In addition, to refer to a point made earlier, the clergy and only the clergy dare have opinions in the Catholic community. Further, clergy and religious control Catholic education, in which one might reasonably expect at least some modest effort at encouraging true creativity. But with the exception of a negligible few, Catholic schools, particularly Catholic colleges, do everything in their power to squelch creativity; they are far more eager to produce dependable wage-earners than a volatile (or so he appears to them) genius who can do so much to embarrass and even cause scandal.

This fear of embarrassment is a stultifying weakness in too much clerical thinking. The non-Catholic world is bad enough with all its atheism, agnosticism, sexualism, and everything else so imperfect and so far outside the Catholic fortress. These monsters we can stand up to, catechism in hand, and expose their badness. There is something so reassuring when the adversary speaks—on whatever subject; we know he is wrong because he isn't on our side. It is another matter when a member of our own club wears the wrong tie or lifts the wrong fork.

The clergy are fearful lest our own human imperfection should ever contradict our well-kept pretense at utter perfection. We protest ardent humility, we demurely lisp *mea culpa, mea culpa;* and when we reach *mea maxima culpa* we achieve the sublime heights of hypocrisy. We don't mean it for a moment. Our every action contradicts this pious ejaculation; we know very well that we are better than others. We are God's anointed, and let's not allow anyone to doubt it for an instant. True, we may affect a pose of liberality in not burning too many books or anathematizing too many of our adversaries, but in reality we are convinced (one might call it invincible conviction) that we are right and everyone else is wrong.

In fact, our conceit is so great that it lacks conviction. We protest too much, which is suspiciously like a tacit admission that we are not quite so convinced as we would like to be. Oh, we feel certain about the Trinity and that sort of thing; after all, God laid that out rather clearly to us a long time ago. What bothers us is all those other areas that don't leap from the New Testament or arise out of an occasional *ex cathedra* comment. Since the artist is a difficult person to get along with—he airs so much dirty linen—it might be better to do away with him altogether. Or if we must have some window dressing to show that we are decent fellows, let's put up a few clerics.

But no dummy in the window really fools anyone.

No. Where there is conviction there is the strength to wrestle with any adversary, whether it be an idea—or merely a rose.

Since the Catholic Church in America will have nothing to do with art, it has fostered artifice in a vain attempt to satisfy the aesthetic needs of its people and also to distract them from the adversary's wares. The sharpest contrast between art and artifice lies in the fact that the former raises questions while the latter provides answers—not tentative answers, but final, irrefutable answers. This is only natural since authoritarians shudder at uncertainties; they breathe easily only in the presence of granite certitude. If for an instant the bishop fumbles an answer, he is convinced that the earth will shatter at his feet and the great red hat will tumble down into the nearest crevice. His people will doubt his divine origins and his infallibility. They will ask further questions. And it must always be remembered that Catholic laymen are not supposed to ask questions. They are born only to listen.

Catholic artifice always has a happy ending. One can almost hear the angels gush their exultation over the sweetness of it all; one can even have visions of cherubim and seraphim singing the only chorus Catholic artifice knows:

> Roses are red,
> Violets are blue.
> I'm going to Rome;
> Why don't you?

8 ❧

A BILL OF PARTICULARS

ONE of the most serious charges that can be brought against the Church in America is its insistence on separate but equal rights in all things, ranging from federal support of its education system to its own propaganda network of newspapers. The Catholic wants to have his cake and eat it too. He demands that he not be discriminated against, and yet he does the very things that bring on discrimination. He wants to be an American, but an American *Catholic*.

Catholicism is a subculture very similar to the subculture that exists in the Negro community. The only real difference is that the Negro has had his shaped for him by whites; the Catholic has chosen his lot. So complete is the Catholic culture that if the rest of the American culture, with all its institutions, were to vanish overnight, a complete watertight Catholic society would still be there the next morning. This is what is known as the Catholic ghetto. Whereas his-

torically Jews and Negroes have been rounded up and
shoved into their ghettos, Catholics righteously and somewhat fearfully built their own, brick by brick, amidst the
sprinkling of holy water.

On reflection, it is strange that Catholics ever came to
America, considering that many of them must have known
about the hostility the country generally showed their religion. But then, one is reminded of the thought expressed
earlier that Catholics are in this country and yet not of it.
We came here, but only on our own terms. In the beginning, possibly, this was not such a bad thing; it did tend to
preserve the faith in the face of the confusion of Protestantism. There can be no argument against defending the faith
from encroachment. What does deserve critical comment is
the process of extension that has resulted in a Catholic subculture so pervasive and so entrenched that a Catholic
scarcely dares wander outside lest he be accused of "passing
over the line."

Few appreciate the enormity of the subculture's influence on the American Catholic, but it is not an exaggeration
to say that many Catholics have lived their entire lives
without once reading a non-Catholic book, subscribing to
a single non-Catholic magazine, going to a movie not officially approved by the bishop, or for that matter having a
personal opinion on politics, education, or sex that did not
originate with either the local pastor or the diocesan newspaper. These people pass their lives without once stepping
outside the Church-oriented welfare state that provides
them with all the necessities from cradle to grave. This has

earned American Catholics the deserved reputation of being a terribly dull and unimaginative lot.

But it is not fair to blame all Catholics for this massive mediocrity; the responsibility rests with the corporate structure, which has seen fit to direct not only their spiritual lives but also their intellectual and cultural as well. The trick—more of a trick of conscience—is that bishops usually convince themselves that all social and cultural matters are part and parcel of the Catholic's spiritual life. While there is a germ of truth in this, it doesn't necessarily justify sterile isolation and self-conscious edification.

Bishops particularly, many of whom are scarcely a generation or two removed from their origins in Ireland, live in sterile isolation. Many of them were born into poor families who had a no-nonsense attitude toward life and who had almost no contact with outsiders. At an early age, often prodded by tradition and eager mothers, the boys went into the seminary, from which in a sense they never emerged. It is no real secret that seminaries are not breeding grounds of pluralism and that they do a pretty thorough job of putting the outside world in its place—beyond the pale. The point is that such men have lived practically all their lives in the tightest ghetto of all and are not about to leave it, probably out of the very human fear of the unknown.

Naturally, this is not said in criticism of the bishops' intentions, which are beyond question, but to reveal the serious defect of the experience many of them share: they are simply unacquainted with society as a whole. They see only a segment of it—the Catholic world; bounded on all sides by Catholic institutions. Needless to say, these institutions are always part of the corporate structure and are thus dominated by bishops and their clerical staffs. This is a most extraordinary state of affairs. The people least qualified by training or disposition to create a culture are the very ones who run the show. It's like appointing a conscientious objector as Secretary of Defense; it simply won't work.

In this country there are over 120 diocesan newspapers. The combined circulation is in the millions, though I suspect the actual readership is less than 20 percent of that. Have you ever actually read a diocesan paper? I don't mean just the headline about the bishop's saying Easter mass (that is what one headline actually said); I mean the entire paper from beginning to end, leaving nothing out—not even the ads for trusses and burial plots.

If the paper isn't listing new clerical appointments, it's describing all the newsworthy activities of the bishop, such as his recent award from the local B'nai B'rith chapter, his accepting a large check from some lay organization, or his laying a cornerstone for a new Catholic Youth Center. Once past the bishop, we read about a recent birth control controversy accompanied by the bishop's fervid condemnation of birth control. Periodically Rome sends something out on the wire, and it takes most of a column to reiterate the Church's position on birth control. This is accompanied by a few remarks by the bishop pointing up the profound wisdom of Rome.

If a Senator says something about federal aid to education, the paper will report it one way or another, depending on the Senator's position. The Superintendent of Education, furrowing his intellectual brow, will plead the case for federal aid to education. Every once in a while a prayer case will come along, and the paper will quote the bishop as saying, "America is becoming more secular every day; thank God for the Catholic Church, and let us all pray for the intentions of the Holy Father."

That is the front page. Week after week after week. Even the bishop's picture never changes.

Inside there are the official notices posted by the bishop. They deal with the fasting and abstinence rules for the season. Once past that sort of thing, we come to the heart of the diocesan newspaper: gossip. We read about the silver jubilee of Sr. Mary Joseph, the *golden* jubilee of Sr. Mary John, and the death of Sr. Mary James, who was only nine weeks shy of *her* golden jubilee. Next to their brief quarter-columns are the half-columns telling the reader about Fr. Francis Xavier O'Brien's twenty-fifth anniversary as pastor of St. Bridget's, along with a kind word from the bishop's office. Several picas away is an item about Fr. Timothy Brannigan, who just got out of the Navy and who has been appointed assistant to Fr. John Sweeny at St. Dominic's. "Father Tim spoke warmly about the Navy but said he was anxious for parish life once more. Father Tim denies any tendency toward *mal de mer*." Still smiling, one reads a full column about the death of Fr. Sean Donovan, who died just nine weeks before *his* golden jubilee and ten days after his thirtieth year as pastor of St. Mary's. The bishop's office tersely comments that a new pastor has not yet been appointed.

There follows the sports page, with its listing of the city all-Catholic teams, and sometimes even an article about some fine young Catholic ballplayer who has made good in the Majors. He is quoted as saying, "I owe a great deal of the credit to my old pastor, Fr. Flynn, who not only showed me how to handle a tough grounder but who also convinced me never to get discouraged. No matter how bad things are, if we stay on God's side, He'll stay on ours." Often some teen-ager will have a sports column about Catholic sports— an inside Catholic sports sort of thing.

The ladies have their page, which reports on various altar groups, sodalities, and similar parochial organizations dedicated to the furtherance of Catholicism in the community. Periodically the bishop appears in their midst, a fixed expression ringed by girlish smiles, as a staff photographer immortalizes an annual banquet at which the bishop accepts a check. Occasionally some fund-raising group presents a pageant or plans a masquerade (come as your favorite saint) for some Catholic charity, all duly reported along with a list of the patronesses, whose spokeswoman promises that *this* year's affair will be even more successful than last year's, which, as everyone recalls, was even more successful than the one before that.

Now that the audience has had its fun and relaxation, the diocesan newspaper sets about the really important business of indoctrination, a page or so that reveals the minds of various priests on such subjects as Church-state relations, the spiritual advantages of being Catholic, more sincere participation in the liturgy, and why Catholics shouldn't marry Protestants and Jews. There may even be a column by a layman announcing to the Catholic community the joys of being a Catholic layman.

Intermingled with this staunch parochialism are wire service stories about the expulsion of several nuns from some country, the papal delegate paying his respects to the new President of Italy, the death of three or four Catholics caught in a remote war, and the latest step in some obscure beatification proceeding. Of course, this business was all reported several weeks earlier in the local secular paper, which headlined the expulsion, explained in detail the problems behind the delegate's six-month delay in paying his respects, and revealed that not only three or four Catholics but also several hundred others were killed. The beatification development was unreported because the editor suspected no one was really interested in an unpronounceable name that had begun its slow ascent in the sixteenth century.

At least once a month the latest ratings of the Legion of Decency are posted, producing a pool or two over what really first-rate foreign movie will make the select list of condemnation next month.

This is the typical diocesan newspaper. There are variations; some run a constant series on smut or the John Birch Society while others retrace Church history in cartoons. Once in a while the papers get a chance to levitate over the appointment of a new bishop or the death of an old pope; but this happens too infrequently to upset the routine of bland repetition that is so central to diocesan publishing one can scarcely tell one edition from another. Only the date changes.

As if this weren't enough to dismay even the most ardent Catholic, we also must face the fact of hierarchical pressure to subscribe. "To be an informed Catholic, read the *Merrimac*." Capping this non sequitur, every parish in the diocese sets aside one Sunday for the poor pastor to admonish his flock to read the local paper, "which alone, in these difficult times, always prints the truth as only a Catholic paper can." Subscription blanks are passed out, along with the stub of a pencil and ushers who wait patiently in the aisle, subtly shuffling the collection basket half-filled with subscriptions. As a slight variation, Catholic children are sent out to ring doorbells with the pastor's blessing and the promise of a little reward (either a soda or a religious medal, depending on the psychology of the pastor) for the boy or girl who brings in the most subscriptions that Sunday afternoon.

The Catholic newspapers are a disgrace to the community and an affront to one's intelligence. Little more than house organs and playthings for bishops and priests who should have more important things to occupy their minds, diocesan newspapers are shamed by secular papers, which, though far less worthwhile then they might be, are infinitely more readable and informative than the best diocesan newspaper.

Diocesan papers are sick for two reasons: they are a written expression of the Catholic ghetto mentality, and they are published by amateurs. But before going into details, a more fundamental issue presents itself: should diocesan newspapers even be published? Or, to put it another way, what function do they serve?

Obviously, the papers are directed at local Catholics. They purport to give the Catholic view on issues, interpret events, and instruct the faithful. But do they do this? What, for example, is the "Catholic view" on events or issues of the day? Strictly speaking, the "Catholic view," that is, the official Catholic position, can only concern itself with faith and morals when set forth *ex cathedra.* What the diocesan paper prints is the local bishop's opinion on things, or what his editor thinks is his opinion. As to instruction, the clerical columns add nothing to what one gets out of a beginner catechism.

About the only thing the paper does is to serve as a bulletin board for the clergy and the Legion of Decency— and as forum for mutual admiration.

Though we can tentatively concede that Catholic communities might once have needed their own newspapers (sort of cousins to local Yiddish or Chinese papers), it is really only honest to admit that they have long outlived whatever usefulness they might once have had. It is about time Catholics grew up and out of their tight little groups. Instead of huddling around the old kerosene lantern, hesitantly tracing out words of episcopal comfort, Catholics should blow the silly thing out and take a long look at themselves and American society.

The diocesan newspapers perpetuate the tradition of Catholic separateness in America. Out of the conviction that Catholic laymen were not to be contaminated by outsiders, both because outsiders were bad and because Catholic laymen were too weak to resist infection, bishops have spent generations and billions of lay dollars to set up their separate but equal institutions. Not only has this corrupted Catholicism and debilitated millions of Catholics, it has prevented proper and mature Catholic participation in the general American community, to the detriment of society because it has thus been denied the influence of Catholic principles. Because of Catholic separateness and the institutions that serve as walls of separation, the Church is misunderstood, feared for its monolithic appearance in religious matters, and mocked for its childish cultural pretensions.

There is only one thing to do about diocesan papers: shut them down, sell the presses, and send the priests out into the world. If all the diocesan newspapers in this country disappeared tomorrow, no one would notice the difference. In a month they would be dimly remembered as some sort of ancient legend like the loony bird or the island of Atlantis. In a year even the legend would be lost in a general fog of indifference.

If it were not for hierarchical coercion, the diocesan papers would have wandered into limbo years ago. But the bishops, who seem to need so many useless appendages to their persons, apparently feel it incumbent upon themselves to carry them on as an old and honorable tradition. They are more than that: a newspaper is as integral a part of a bishop's office as the episcopal ring and pectoral cross. Though a bishop may feel his paper adds something to his office, it doesn't, simply because, despite all his efforts, only a small percentage of Catholics (though large in national numerical totals) subscribe to the paper, much less actually read it or even glance at it.

The ubiquitous diocesan newspapers, in addition to serving no useful purpose in the Catholic community, are derelict in another way. By perpetuating a lost cause, they engage the talents of thousands whose presence would be far more significant elsewhere. Priests should not be editors of newspapers, just as they shouldn't be superintendents of schools. Their employment as both is a scandal and a misuse of sacramental power; they should be *priests*. The rest of the newspaper staffs, instead of huddling in a tight little Catholic circle of mutual back-patting and splendid security, should be dispersed into the American newspaper world. We complain so much about American society, but it never seems to occur to us to do anything about it except cling more tightly together in horror at "all those others." This state is assuredly very un-Christian and contrary to our Lord's admonition to go out into the world. We are missionaries, at least in theory. What we actually are and do is a different matter altogether. Rather than go out, we turn in on ourselves; rather than be missionaries, we live complacently in our ghetto. We just don't want to get our hands dirty.

Catholics in newspaper work would be doing far more for the Church and humanity by acting as a leavening force in the general American newspaper profession. But tradition being what it is, we can scarcely expect change, and the paper that the bishop inherits will continue putting out the regular edition each week. It is built into the system.

There is also another explanation. The present bishops, with few exceptions, were born while this country was still mission territory, or shortly thereafter. They grew up among millions of Catholic immigrants who could scarcely speak the English language and who were totally bewild-

ered by the mad events of World War I and the period of
the Lost Generation. Critically important is the fact that
their basic attitudes were formed half a century ago, along
with the usual prejudices and predilections. Today, living
entirely in a Catholic environment, they often don't see the
modern world as it actually is. The age of clever atheism is
largely gone; America is searching for meaning; yet the
Catholic community, with so much to offer, turns in on
itself just as it did in the early 1900s.

Most bishops, without really thinking about it, assume
that a diocesan paper is as necessary today as it was when
they were boys. This just isn't so any more. Diocesan papers
don't report news; the general papers do. Diocesan papers
don't interpret or analyze; they merely repeat the same old
Catholic positions on the same old social problems week
after week. Besides, there are hundreds of Catholic magazines that likewise cover the same old social problems issue
after issue. Diocesan papers do not instruct their readers in
theology and philosophy, nor do they develop a strong
"Catholic mentality" by presenting good counsel; the devotional pages carry the same blustering apologetics that
were popular a generation or so ago.

Some day some bishop is going to take a good, objective look at his local paper and he is going to stop this nonsense. He knows he doesn't really need a paper to communicate with the clergy and the laity. He has the telephone for
the one and pastoral letters for the others.

If despite all this a bishop still wants a paper, then for
heaven's sake let him publish a *real* paper by putting it in
the hands of competent professionals. Let him hire an ex-

pert layman, lay down basic policy, and then get out of the editor's office and allow a real newspaperman to run the show. Any paper worth its salt has an editorial policy about local or national events. Let the Catholic papers take stands on politics, local issues, and international controversies. Let the Catholic press *stand* for something besides pious drivel. Newspapers are no place for homilies and pedagogic instruction; they are supposed to be engaged in what concerns the community. Let the Catholic paper stop constantly talking to a mere handful of devout Catholics and address itself to the entire community; let it battle with the secular press and secular ideas. *Let it do something!*

Unfortunately, this will never happen. We want only to be liked, not respected; we want to whisper among ourselves, not talk forthrightly with others who might not agree with us. We accommodate ourselves much as the Negroes have been required to accommodate themselves to white supremacy. Just as the Negroes are beginning to change, to protest the degrading principle of accommodation, so too should the Catholics. But we won't.

Under the guise of prudence, too many bishops remain silent on all matters that are not directly related to birth control, abortion, smut, and federal aid to education. There they are on safe ground because everybody knows the Church's position before the bishop even speaks. To the rest of the world the bishop is an old crank who hasn't changed his press releases for twenty years. The Catholic, faced by outside silence, mistakes contempt for affection; the bishop mistakes unresponsiveness for approval. If the bishops want a lesson in journalism, let them look at *The Christian Science Monitor*.

Practically everything said about Catholic newspapers can be said about the great majority of Catholic magazines, particularly those under religious editorship.

Catholic magazines may be divided into three categories. First are the clearly devotional, published by religious orders, which either support the principles of the order or promote a particular cult. These magazines are private and special-purpose publications which shouldn't be embarrassed by outside opinion. Second, with some exceptions, are the periodicals which are published by either the secular clergy or an order and which purport to be topical or cultural. In the third group are the few magazines published by laymen plus the exceptions from the second group.

Two characteristics typify Catholic magazines of the second group: they are complacent and they are dull. Those that aim to be topical repeat the faults of diocesan newspapers; they merely restate, issue after issue, the traditional position of the Church on the standard moral question, federal aid to education, the correctness of Catholic belief, and more recently ecumenism and racial justice.

There is something Olympian about their pronouncements that borders on condescension of the rudest sort. Their principal purpose is to reassure Catholics that the various editors have matters well under control and that everyone can sleep comfortably that night. They fail to go beyond the safety and security that mark virtually all Catholic public expressions. Catholics never argue; they pontificate, and in the dreariest tones conceivable. The people who put out these magazines, again, are of course amateurs; they are no more true editors than the clerics who pump out the diocesan newspapers. Also perpetuating the dogged principle of Catholic separateness, they merely reinforce the pathetic boundaries of the Catholic ghetto. These publications are such limp imitations of the national periodicals; and yet, with almost boyish enthusiasm, hundreds of priests promote in their pages the myth that Catholics are somehow distinct from and superior to the rest of society.

It is all utter nonsense. This insistence, this error, and this pallid world should cease. If the Catholic segment of society must have its own little journals of opinion and culture, then let us set about writing them honestly and with the proper sort of talent.

The more wretched aspect of the second group's efforts is its so-called cultural publishing. Poetry that would put the worst amateur to shame and fiction that is nothing but thinly disguised sermons are the extent of the magazines' creativity. Their acts of criticism are more acts of barbarism and their displays of art are straight out of a third-grade classroom. In fact, these magazines are propaganda manuals intended to distract millions of Catholics and delude them into thinking that the fare printed in their pages is a worthy substitute for the pernicious evil published elsewhere. In all candor, these magazines reflect the cultural limitations of their clerical editors, not the cultural aspirations of Catholics in America. As long as these editors continue to run the periodicals, we will be inundated with a mediocrity that is a humiliation to Church members and a never-ending source of amused contempt to the rest of society.

The cause is clear. The editors are in the same frame of mind as the bishops who publish newspapers; they don't have the necessary cultural background, and they can't see beyond the narrow limits of their ghetto. They consider as works of art a miserable poem praising God or a story that glibly presents a death-bed conversion (with scarcely any struggle at all), both of a literary quality fit only for junior-high-school English classes. They aren't art. They are propaganda tracts. All cultural matters in these magazines inevitably refer to something specifically Catholic and inevitably expose the grotesque conviction that if it weren't for Rome, civilization would have perished long ago.

In criticism, the writers praise their fellow priests who produce the worst trash and, in mock charity, gently chastise everything else. Even where they strain to praise dimly an outsider's work, they nevertheless leave subtle doubts as to the author's intelligence or integrity. About things Catholic they see only the Catholicity, in doctrinal or affiliative terms; they never question quality. If a work is by a Catholic and about a Catholic, it is approved whether or not it has any genuine merit at all.

In brief, the magazines are out to promote Catholicism, not literature or art or criticism. It is for this reason that they are shams, and it is also for this reason that no one outside the dim corridors of the Catholic cultural ghetto will even glance at them.

The solution? Along with diocesan papers, shut them

all down, send the priests out to their real vocations, and disperse all the laity into the general publishing field. Catholics some day will simply have to get out of their safe little ghettos and face the real demand to do something affirmative about society as a whole. For generations they have turned their backs on those who desperately need their influence; for generations they have preferred not to dirty their hands or their minds. It is so comfortable to turn out pious pap that does nothing for anyone. It is like preaching the American dream to the board of directors of General Motors. But the Catholic message will be carried to the world only if Catholics go out into the world.

There is the third group of magazines, published by laymen. There are no more than a handful, and they suffer from particular disabilities that only serve to expose the false premise of Catholic publishing.

The greatest disability is the fact that much of the hierarchy is instinctively against them. Here, as in all things, members of the corporate structure feel safe only when some easily manipulated cleric is running the show. That way lies safety; there will be no risk of embarrassment. Despite the opposition, there are a few rather determined people who see Catholicism as a dynamic force with a great potential for affecting society. *Commonweal* is the only respectable Catholic magazine dealing with current events. And it is the only such magazine respected outside the Catholic community. True, *America* is often commented upon by the secular press, but primarily because it is a magazine published by Jesuits, and non-Catholics always seem to assume that Jesuits speak for the Church. *Com-*

monweal has the well-earned enmity of much of the hierarchy, and there is even one cardinal archbishop who won't
allow it in his seminary. *Commonweal's* stature rests on its
editorial policy of looking at events and issues, not for a
bishop's nod of approval.

There are a number of worthwhile magazines throughout the Catholic publishing world, including a number of
clerically run publications, but they are in such a small minority as to cause scarcely a ripple. For example, *Jubilee* and
The Critic do very good work in their fields. However, these
two magazines have small circulations and are distributed
almost exclusively within the Catholic subculture, so that
they are hardly known among the bulk of Catholics and are
virtually unknown outside. The consequence is that though
they are worthwhile, they have almost no audience. This is
a devastating commentary on Catholic publishing—two
good magazines with almost no readership, either in or out
of the Catholic community. In contrast with these are a
number of Catholic magazines, published by clerics, which
have circulations ranging from 150,000 to 700,000 and
which are vastly inferior. They lack any incisiveness at all,
and their tone is always pietistic. Visually they are an embarrassment and intellectually they are an insult. But they
flourish, and, unhappily, they appear to fulfill the reading
needs of Catholics.

There are approximately 43,000,000 Catholics in this
country. Is it possible that only 10,000 or 20,000 are up to
the fare of *Jubilee, The Critic,* and *Commonweal?* The fact
is that hundreds of thousands of Catholics read, but they do
not read Catholic magazines. Disdaining the pallid outpour-

ing of the Catholic press, they read secular magazines like *The New Yorker, Atlantic Monthly, Saturday Review,* and *Harper's.* If the Catholic press is going to win these readers over, it must provide them with something worthwhile. This is most unlikely, of course, since the clerically run publications will remain what they are—safe, tedious, predictable, and editorially oriented to a perpetuation of the Catholic cultural ghetto.

The few lay publications, like the ones I have mentioned, will never gain a large Catholic audience (to say nothing of a respectable non-Catholic audience), because they lack the implied imprimatur that the vast majority of Catholics need to reassure them that this sort of thing is pleasing to the local pastor or bishop. The lay publications are underfinanced, understaffed, and underread, all of which is a tragedy since any honest comparison between them and the clerically published magazines reveals the undeniable superiority of the former. If we must have a subculture, let it rest upon talent and not upon utter mediocrity.

To effect a change, to bring something to the rest of society, will require two things: the dissolution of the Catholic subculture and the construction of a genuine culture based on Christian concepts expressed in modern, affirmative terms. As it is, this thing called a Catholic subculture consists of a series of negations. It has taken all the ingredients of American culture and tested them against ancient fears and prejudices, distilling out all those that caused Catholics the least bit of uneasiness. What remains is the Catholic subculture, a sickly monster, too weak to live and too strong to die.

9 ❧

TERRAE INCOGNITAE

IF literature is to be considered art, it must encompass the whole of man, not just those portions that serve a particular purpose or advance a particular argument. The history of literature—especially in the last century or so— shows a consistent tendency on the part of writers to prostitute the art and make it serve as a vehicle for special pleading. Propagandists, mindful that emotional involvement helps a cause far more than intellectual niceties, have always used literature, whether prose or poetry, to their own ends. Dictators have always had their stables of literary panderers who have sought to join together the will of the dictator and the allegiance of the people.

In America, every scrambling idea has its promoters who turn literature into a bawd to promote social doctrines, political interests, economic principles, and anything else that catches the public eye momentarily. We have our chauvinistic novels during wars and our antiwar novels between wars. In the 1930s we had our angry protest literature, directed against big business, the state, capitalism, religion, law, medicine, and chastity. Its writers invaded the publishing field, the theater, radio, and the movie industry. With so much effort expended, it would seem that this great body of propaganda would have had a noticeable effect on the national community. Such was not the case, however, for two simple reasons: it was negative, that is, it was *against* something, never *for* something; and it failed to encompass all of man, showing him rather as an economic or social or political or sexual automaton.

Art consists in affirmations, which propaganda lacks completely. Once the particular cause passes away, its supportive literature becomes embarrassing. It would be nonsensical to say that the artist shouldn't bring certain convictions to his work, for the artist's conviction, or vision, is precisely what impels him to create. It is essential, however, that the artist not cheat. He shouldn't merely present the particular facet of man that will serve his purposes. For example, in the protest literature of the 1930s, was there ever a weak or dishonest proletarian or an honest politician? Was war anything but a profit-making operation of the munition makers or religion a device for exploiting the downtrodden?

Whereas the writers of the 1930s produced their own sort of violent and committed literature, the 1940s, both during and after the war, saw writing preoccupied first with winning the war and man's inhumanity in warfare and, later, with pleasant reflections on having come through alive. The 1950s and what we have of the 1960s are characterized by an absence of definition. No one can really say which way literature is going today because no one really knows which way society is going.

The most obvious mark of recent literature is its tendency to portray man as alienated, alone, afraid. It lacks commitment. And it fails to encompass the whole man, most often because its dominant trait is hopelessness. Through the millennia, man has hoped for so much; and since the final collapse of his dreams, man has lost all hope. In a way, man can hardly be blamed for this what I hope will be temporary despair. Most writers today are not religiously oriented; they can't imagine God as sovereign over our ugly and corrupt world. If they suspect God exists, they hate Him. Either way, God doesn't fit into their world. This is the alienation that permeates so much of modern literature. There is so much talk about the breakdown of communication between people; this isn't the problem at all. The problem lies in the fact that there is nothing to say.

Viewed naturalistically, what can one man communicate to another? There is no God; that is, death ends everything. There is no assurance that civilization has a future because of the constant threat of thermonuclear warfare. All man knows is the *now* of things. Even the past is not fixed; histories change as attitudes change. What really caused World Wars I and II? What or who was really responsible for the Protestant Reformation? Was Napoleon a hero or a villain? Was Shakespeare Bacon or someone else? Was Jesus the Christ or just a remarkably decent Jew Who spoke well from boats? Is the universe in a static state or in flux?

The world is so thoroughly confused we don't even know our friends from our enemies. Once we were good and everyone else was bad, but propagandists have unsettled that prior certainty by exposing all our evils and shortcomings. History can be so written that one can't say who actually won World War II, despite the fact that I've always *known* the United States won both world wars quite on its own. I remember as a small child being utterly chagrined one day to learn that the United States wasn't the largest country in the world. I was more than chagrined; I was humiliated. And today, the thought that Tokyo is bigger than New York is a constant source of embarrassment, as is the fact that Russia has a more powerful rocket propulsion system.

For the last fifteen years or so I have been instructed both to fear and to hate the Russians. But now, with "the yellow peril rising out of the East," I am being told, albeit tentatively, that the day may come when the two great nations of Russia and the United States will be fighting side by side against the Red Chinese. I am told further that if things keep going the way they are "populationwise," in several generations we will all be standing cheek by jowl with not even enough room to sit down. Unemployment is on the increase, our gold reserve is way down, machines are replacing men, and scientists are perfecting a device that will destroy life but won't so much as scratch buildings.

We have no future, we have no past; only the now. And this now is populated by billions who cannot communicate from one island of fear to another. It is no longer true that no man is an island. *Every man is an island.* And each island is getting smaller and smaller.

Once man felt himself both unique and potent. Today

he is a cipher and impotent. Once there were horizons and mystery. Today there is only the now. We have the state over us and we watch it move through time and we have no way to alter its course by so much as a hair's breadth. We vote—or some of us do—but what difference does it make who is President when the state, as if obeying some hidden magnetic attraction, creeps on in time to what we all know lies in wait—extinction, whether tomorrow or a thousand years hence? And then there is always the bomb. We labor, and the state charges us for the bombs we don't want. We take tranquilizers in the vain hope of sleep, but there is no sleep, just a vague twilight state where our fancies become nightmares that bridge the span from this now to the next now. We see life becoming more synthetic, from a loaf of bread that isn't bread to national ideals that aren't ideals but rather unavoidable catastrophes.

And huddled on his own little island crouches each man, waiting, waiting, waiting for the end. Will it be with a bang? Or will it be an endless sameness? Do we have a dreadful fear of change or an equally dreadful fear of no change? What of my children? I sometimes dream of their future—their plans (really mine), careers, marriages—and wonder if they will someday dream as I do now. But will there even be a time when they, too, can dream? Or marry, or have careers? There may not *be* a tomorrow. And if there is, won't it be merely an extension of the present with all its sameness and fears?

I can be certain of only one thing: *now*. This is the only certainty when man lives on the natural level alone.

In opposition is the supernatural view of life. And it is

this view, as held by Christians, that gives man both a past and a future. The past begins with God and the future ends with God. In between we have the life we lead on earth. We have Christ in our past and we have Him in our future. We need to bring Him into our *now*.

But Christ doesn't just reside in the tabernacle, nor does His Spirit breathe solely on philosophical and theological writings. Christ belongs in the market place, at the crossroads, in the drawing room, and in the bedroom. But Christ can't go to these places unless we take Him. It is true that we are His only hands, but it is equally true that we are His feet and His voice. If we are still, He is still; if we are silent, He is silent.

The greatest absence in the world today is of Christ in the market place, and the second greatest absence in the world today, which causes the first, is of the Church in the market place. Nowhere is this truer than in America.

Catholics in this country have always shown a marked preference for their own kind. It is very reassuring to ring one's life with dependability, to know that one's views are shared and one's prejudices reinforced by the subcommunity at large. Most attractive is the assurance that one will never have to engage in controversy or, what is worse, occasionally be proved wrong. This is not to say that Catholics don't offer criticism; indeed, quite the opposite. Catholics are particularly noted for their tendency to criticize others. That is why we have so many Catholic newspapers, Catholic magazines, and Catholic books. From our cloister we preach, ostensibly among ourselves but actually to the world beyond the reaches of our tight little ghetto. Further, we do so on our own terms and without bothering to listen to a rejoinder. Occasionally we will invite an outsider to engage in what purports to be a "dialogue," but we make certain that the guest is essentially harmless and that he knows our ground rules of discussion.

However, Catholics will not go out into the national community and engage in open controversy and debate. The clergy are directed by the hierarchy not to, and the laity are disowned if they presume to. (By *disowned,* I mean the formal statement by the local bishop that the layman in question, "of course, doesn't speak for the Church; he only presents his personal opinions, which are not necessarily consonant with or contrary to the Church's views.")

Some years ago a new musical opened on Broadway and was reviewed by Walter Kerr. Later asked for an opinion of Mr. Kerr's review, one of the principals remarked, "You know what Kerr thinks. After all, he's a Catholic. What else could he say?" Once in a while a cleric will appear on a television discussion on, say, the population explosion, Church-state relations, federal aid to education, or psychiatry and modern society. Before you even sit down to watch you know two things: one, precisely where the cleric stands, and two, that he will say very little. As to newspaper exposures, clerics never speak directly; their remarks always come from a spokesman, that is, they present a carefully prepared press release which has passed the bishop's censor.

No. Catholics prefer to take their ease in congenial surroundings. The suspicion arises that we consider the present scene so transitory as to dissolve into insignificance. After all, the Church has been around for two thousand years, and, by Christ's promise, will be here long after everyone else and their wretched institutions have crumbled into dust. While this may be true, it doesn't justify a clean-hands policy of isolation and self-sterilization, which in fact violates Christ's admonition to go into the world, not to feast in the privacy of the cenacle.

If society is in dire circumstances, then it is the obligation of the Church to go out to society and do what it can to help it out of its misery. If, instead of insulating itself, the Catholic community had years ago gone out of its ghetto and into the market place, it is very likely that things would be far better today than they are. Explicitly, society is lacking any awareness of the spiritual nature of man. This is precisely the gift that Catholics can bring to the rest of mankind. And in a way we do this, but because of a fatal flaw we lose out all the time.

What destroys our efforts to reaffirm the spirituality of man is the fact that we talk about spirit and nothing else, as if man were by nature a disembodied spirit encased in a foul prison called the body. Theologically and philosophically Catholics don't officially believe that, but humanly and culturally they do.

Anyone at all familiar with the Catholic cultural scene knows that it is incapable of producing art. Once it did, but not any more, particularly in this country where Catholic puritanism has vastly exceeded the brand brought over by the Protestants. It's almost as if this excess were a sign of ultrapatriotism as well as a Catholic reassurance that we are eminently trustworthy.

In a sense, all this is little more than part of the never-ending battle between Protestants and Catholics. If Protestants stress the Bible, we will stress tradition; if Protestants encourage clerical marriage, we will forbid it; if Protestants believe in the private interpretation of Scripture, we will deny it; if Protestants are moderate Christians, we will be extremists; if Protestants relax their puritanism, we will tighten it; if Protestants slowly evolve a naturalistic or social philosophy, we slowly evolve a supernaturalistic and antisocial philosophy; if Protestants liberalize sex, we preach greater and greater austerity (virginity is the better and more holy state); if Protestants occupy the market place, we won't even come into town. So fantastic is our position that it wasn't until early 1963 that the highest Catholic, Protestant, and Jewish official representatives met in an interfaith gathering, the occasion being the Chicago Conference on Race and Religion. It took over four hundred years for this first breakdown.

It is because the Catholics have isolated themselves that they have isolated culture from reality, producing, as I have said, a subculture concerned exclusively with the spirit. This is quite a human thing to do, really. When a man concentrates on spirituality, he need not concern himself with the person. That is, he can sacrifice the person to the end sought—salvation. Since the Catholic is convinced he is right about salvation (with the corollary that everyone else is wrong), he wants all others to believe as he believes, even if it takes the Inquisition. But corporal force has nasty side effects and runs the risk of being un-Christian.

The safest thing to do is ignore the person completely

and talk endlessly about salvation. Then no one can call you un-Christian. However, not only does this ignore one-half of the man we are trying to push into heaven; it also invalidates such practices as corporal acts of mercy and absolutely violates the conscience of all but the most pre-sumptuously proud. Another weakness of this attitude is that it is man-to-God oriented, which is good as far as it goes but which ignores the commandment to love our neighbor.

Catholic culture paints a false picture of man. It grudg-ingly admits the existence of the body but all the while denies its presence. It acknowledges sin pretty much as some people acknowledge a poor relation. But one never invites that sort into one's home. The Catholic mentality will acknowledge a vague awareness of human psychology, but as if it were more an example of invincible ignorance than truth. Catholic culture will admit the value of art, but only if it will lead everyone directly to Rome. ("Do not pass Go, do not collect $200"—that sort of thing.)

The American Catholic cannot stop being self-con-scious about his Catholicity long enough to be authentically Catholic. He always contrasts himself sharply with non-Catholics. "Of course, you allow divorce; we don't. . . . Naturally, I condemn immorality. I'm a Catholic. . . . We have seven children. Yes, we're Catholic. . . . Bingo? What's wrong with Bingo? . . . Of course *America* gave it a bad review. The man and woman weren't even married! . . . Do you think you really ought to take her to the dance? She's not Catholic, dear. . . . Faulkner was a dirty writer; no Catholic would write such things. . . . I don't care if they do call it art, no decent woman would pose without clothes on. . . . Sex? Sex? What's that?"

Now, then, what about sex? For one thing, no matter how we try to wriggle out of it, sex is here to stay. It is just as much a part of life as original sin, and each affects us all pretty much the same way. We can't get away from either, though various of us try to misplace or ignore one or both. There are some who blame original sin for everything, just as others blame sex. Indeed, some equate the two, and wish Eve had paid less attention to the tree and more to her attire. Not a few breathe a sigh of relief thinking about their baptism, as if that settled everything, just as others, when they take the vows, thank God they've gotten rid of sex for all time.

However, while original sin is actually a bad thing, sex isn't. Original sin is a deprivation, an obstacle to eternal life, and in addition is the cause of all our earthly suffering. It is death. Sex, on the other hand, is a beginning, a gateway. It is life. Both life and death let loose terrible possibilities for each of us, of course, depending on how we approach them. One thing is certain: we could all do without original sin, but not without sex.

A priest talking to a group of teen-agers about sex once drew an interesting analogy with the consecration of the host at mass. He said that while it is perfectly all right for the priest to hold the host, it would be terribly wrong for one of the teen-agers present to do what the priest legitimately can do. The same thing is true about sex. Marriage confers permission to do what would otherwise be a transgression. Having given a proper perspective to the matter of legitimacy, the priest went on with the conference, quite convinced he had made a rather useful comparison that would surely help determine the sex life of the teen-agers.

In the same vein are various Catholic books, mostly written by priests, that set out to instruct the laity on sex. Most modern efforts, happily, no longer dwell on the eternal mystery of procreation as if sex consisted solely in married females giving birth to babies. Today our more advanced sex manuals have brought the birth of babies into its normal relationship to the sexual act; they make it quite clear that babies *result* from the sexual act, much as water is produced when two molecules of hydrogen combine with one molecule of oxygen. While few denigrate sexual intercourse, they still tend to present it as a rather doubtful means to an end, the implication being that they wish God had planned it otherwise—for example, by a certain form of prayer or a writ issued by the chancery. Sex is portrayed as being a studied physical activity leaving the mind free to meditate on the moral good of tithing. What none of them ever reveal is that sexual intercourse is probably the most pleasurable experience man will ever know. Put another way, sex is a lot of fun, the various Catholic manuals to the contrary notwithstanding. If it weren't, the earth would be bare.

God, Who is far wiser than the promoters of didactic sex, wanted to assure the perpetuation of man, and did so by giving man the delightful activity of sexual intercourse. Imagine what things would be like if sex were an experience as neutral as mowing the lawn or as tedious as adding up a long column of figures. And yet, being both pleasurable and consequential, it must not be abused. Because gluttony does not produce ulcers doesn't reduce the seriousness of the offense, and because dropping bombs may give no real pleasure doesn't minimize the consequences of the act. Sex is a combination of pleasure and possible consequences. In truth, with increased frequency there is a definite increase in the possibility of consequences as well as a risk of a decrease in pleasure. It is a matter of proportion.

But proportion isn't what our clerical pedagogues stress, and for a simple reason, I think. They are mostly strangers to sex. Truly, it is just as presumptuous for a priest to talk about sex as it is for a layman to talk about religious vows. In attempting to analyze something central to the other's state, each lacks the insight that comes with experience. That state is something visceral, something that must be lived before it can be understood. I remember once trying to explain what it was like to be overseas in the last war. My listener, who had only read about the war, understood to a certain extent, with his mind. What was missing was his emotional presence. This is the fate of the celibate who tries to understand the nature of sex. Although he may place sex in Christian society, he cannot place sex in man's life. I suffer an equal disability in attempting to discuss a priest's celibacy. My mind may function well, but I lack emotional presence.

It is important to realize that sex is not Christian. It is a power, an instinctive drive, natural to man. You cannot Christianize sex; you must Christianize man. The error lies in trying to change sex from what it is to what some people wish it were. You cannot change sex; you can only change man. That is why so much contemporary talk about sex is useless. The speakers fail to look clearly at sex, trying instead to pretend that sex is something else. It would be equally mad to try to deform a square into a circle or a truth into a lie. No matter how we attempt to bend sex one way or another, it will snap back into place, unchanged and ever potent. What happens when we try to bend it is that man breaks down into licentiousness or breaks up in terrified impotence. We need a Christian approach to sex, not a retreat from it.

In terms of culture, modern man seems either to approach sex as if it were all there was or to say that life is anything *but* sex. The former, if labels are necessary, is the hedonist, while the latter is the Christian. Actually, the Christian position contains a subsidiary dichotomy, with some Protestants holding that sex may be enjoyed without regard to consequences, that is, sexual relations, if adequately prepared for, can be entered into irresponsibly; and with *most* Catholics insisting that one must accept the responsibility for one's sexual actions without placing an artificial obstruction between cause and effect.

Regardless of this procedural contradiction, the Christian in modern society can't really adjust to sex. This is partly owing to our Puritan heritage and partly a reaction to the hedonist principle. Protestants and Catholics share the fallacy of wishing the *difficulties* of sex away while still retaining sex itself. I don't think it is entirely unfair to conclude that many Protestants want sex without the consequences and many Catholics want the consequences without sex. To *this* Protestant, sex becomes an end in itself; to *this* Catholic, sex becomes a means to an end, not in the traditional biological sense of creating life but as a means to damnation.

We Catholics, who have a way of outdoing everyone else once we put our minds to it, have actually canonized Alphonsus Liguori (1696–1787) who proclaimed, very seriously and with purported proofs, that more souls are in hell because of sins of sex than for any other kind. As has been observed, how could he know who was and who wasn't in hell? Besides, is sexual transgression as bad as so many profess? Is it really as bad as a willful act of pride or avarice when one realizes that sexual transgression is an erroneous extension of a thoroughly human instinct while pride and avarice are a denial of man's natural instinct to love? It must be remembered that the angels fell through pride, not sex. Our Lord Himself condemned pride far more vehemently than he did the woman taken in adultery.

This is intended to be not a justification for sexual abuses but rather an effort to put sex in its proper perspective. While our Lord refused to condemn the woman taken in adultery, he didn't leave it at that (as so many moderns wish to believe). He admonished her, "Go thy way and sin no more."

The act of sexual intercourse cannot be approached as if it were some sort of sacrament, despite the pious sexual admonitions in Catholic manuals. Sex is sex and intercourse is intercourse, which is a physical activity, not a spiritual communion. It is really more similar to eating or any other physical activity than to praying or meditating. Eating, if we were to imagine a peculiar culture, could have all sorts of mystical and sacramental implications, each ingestion might be considered as the ingestion of God's grace, but only when one's stomach was free from befouling bloat; otherwise, it would be a desecration. Sleeping could end up being a tricky business if it involved the spiritual detail of lying only on one's left side.

What distinguishes sexual intercourse from other physical activities is the host of consequences that flow from it and the social circumstances that surround it. What would the situation be if intercourse had nothing to do with procreation, but rather had the same lack of physical consequences as ordinary handshaking? Similarly, what if the participants had no special relationship but merely knew each other as indifferently as two people at a concert? The point is, we must see the activity as it is before we can begin to place it in its context; that is, sexual intercourse (or for that matter any sexual activity from simple kissing to the most perverted complexity) must be recognized as an *action* in and of itself.

However, the act is not isolated and does not lack consequences. Without enlarging on the details, which all Catholics are aware of, I wish to re-emphasize the need not to confuse sexual intercourse with everything that surrounds it. Our problems today arise from this confusion and from the fact that the word *sex* has come to include everything from the first look between lovers to the final farewell. Since even an innocent smile may lead to sexual intercourse, it is far better not to smile unless one is securely married and approaches the marriage bed with the spiritual aspirations one brings to the communion rail.

Viewed from another perspective, what really causes

the difficulty about sex is not the surroundings or the consequences, neither of which has even a particle of the attraction that venereal pleasure has for mankind. If sexual activity weren't so thoroughly appealing and exciting, there would be little need to fence so endlessly with it. The tree wasn't Eve's problem; it was the fruit.

Sexual activity produces pleasure, whether we are talking about sexual intercourse, masturbation, or sodomy. However, our approving of one only, any two, or all three depends on surroundings. In this connection Christianity plays a pivotal role. It is a basic Christian principle that one's sex life should consist of sexual intercourse with one's spouse alone. It is a Catholic principle that no artifical means may be used to prevent the possible consequence of pregnancy resulting from the act. And no other sexual activity is permitted, even if one is sorely tempted.

These principles are part of our culture in the same way as monogamy and varying ages of consent. In a word, they are on the books, like the laws against stealing. Actually, official sexual morality is more like the Eighteenth Amendment, which attempted to prohibit drinking; and everyone knows what a dismal failure that was. The reason was obvious except to the few fanatics who thought that all you had to do to change human nature was emend the Constitution. What might have originated as an expression of moral principle ended as a farce because a large segment of the public laughingly and openly defied the law and most public officials did almost nothing to enforce it. The result was corruption, crime, and cynicism. Finally, everyone realized the silliness of it all and threw the amendment out.

Isn't that pretty much what is presently happening to sexual morality? We have the law, but a large segment of society, aided and abetted by indifferent moral arbiters, is striving with considerable success to have the law thrown out. In a way, these people can't be blamed because they don't really know what they are doing. The breakdown is not in terms of sex but in terms of Christianity. As I said before, you cannot Christianize sex; you must Christianize man, the possessor of the sexual power. Lacking some defined religious or philosophical context, sex has no meaning beyond the fact that it is pleasurable. If there is no purpose to life, how can one phase of it have purpose? If life is a catch-as-catch-can proposition, why not grab all you can get *now*, not at some hypothetical moment in the future? Besides, who knows there will be a tomorrow? *All we know is now.*

While still possessing some vestiges of an earlier Christian culture, American culture today is very very close to being non-Christian; that is, it incorporates almost no affirmative Christian principles. The usual method of proving such a charge would be to talk about various standard indicia like marriage, chastity, divorce, political ethics, and business practices. More helpful will be a brief look at the three theological virtues—faith, hope, and charity.

Faith in America? We lost that when we filled out all our frontiers and were forced to look at ourselves instead of distant horizons. The only faith we have is our faith in—or resignation to—our power to destroy. So pointless have we become that President Eisenhower actually had to form a committee of distinguished Americans to try to define our national goals. These men only added to the confusion. Our writers, from Papa Hemingway to the anonymous television hack, have reduced America to the level of a bad joke. And the people? They cheat on their income taxes, lie their way out of jury duty, and steal grapes at the supermarket. There are those who have faith in America, but their timid voices speak out only to their most reliable dependents.

The lack of faith in America arises out of a lack of faith in God. And if one thing is certain about this country's culture, it is that God is absent from it. This goes beyond a few decisions of the Supreme Cout on prayers in public schools; it goes to the basic matter of social behavior itself. God in the market place is an absurdity, a contradiction in terms. In a way we should be glad of this, because even more grotesque would *be* God in the market place, particularly since the God brought over to this country by the Puritans is the very God any thinking person would drive not only out of the market place but out of the country.*

This God was a blasphemous imitation of the true God. He was the God of vengeance, the hell-fire and brimstone beast who meted out damnation to anyone who so much as smiled. He was against everything—music, dancing, smoking, sex, art, literature, plays, beauty, humor, and anything

---

* The Puritan God I refer to has no relationship to the Christian God worshiped by Catholics and Protestants alike. The Puritan God, as I use the term, refers to a caricature that was instilled in the popular mind by such forces as religious extremism, earlier American writers, and American mythology. This God became a dominant image in American society when the true principles of Protestantism and Catholicism were put aside by the majority of the American people, who, though possibly giving lip service to traditional religion, constructed one of their own in order to justify their ethics.

else that made life happy and pleasant. He approved of sharp business practices, slavery, harsh punishments, social injustice, vested interests, the crushing of labor, and everything else that made life wretched and mean.

The nation grew up with that God. We can be thankful that he has been driven from the market place, and we should pray that he will be driven out of his last hiding place, the human heart.

In their rage, the writers and commentators not only drove *that* God away but also made it practically impossible for a replacement to fill the void. The result is a no-God's-land where everyone moves about in eccentric circles, their eyes downcast as if they were vaguely searching for something they suspect is missing.

Hope? There is no hope without faith. And that is why ours is a culture of despair. Despair has crept in more and more as faith has crept out of our lives. Our writers, our painters, our composers, our critics and commentators all reflect this. Hope is founded on the possibility of change, specifically change for the better. We might hope that somehow this nation, or God, will lift us up to something better. And we could make the effort instead of merely presuming on the goodness of the state or of God. But what's the use? The state isn't even aware of us, and God— there is no God. Nothing will change except to get worse.

Charity? Even the word has been corrupted by abuse. Charity is for those too shiftless to take care of themselves. Charity is the money paid out to avoid becoming involved. A check, a dime in some ugly beggar's cup, and on to the club. But what if we substitute *Love?* Love is license; love is sex; love is a tear in the eye, soft music, a poignant death scene. Love is not interfering with the dope addict or the homosexual. Love is letting the suicide work out his own destiny. Love is what the drunken philosopher tells the youngsters to make. Love is—being left alone. Love is hating the cop who pulls in a pusher. Love is cheating the boss and splitting with the labor agitator. Love is winking at another man's wife. Love is reasonable alimony and child support. Love is dirty pictures handed to children. Love is a tenement. Love is a restrictive covenant. Love is a loud noise on Saturday night. Love is—nothing.

For that matter, who is there to love? Not my neighbor who is a liar, a thief, a hypocrite, a coward, a fornicator. I can only love the right sort of man, someone congenial, clever, successful; in short, someone like myself. That is why I am so alone. If only *one* person could honestly say he loved my neighbor, possibly then I might do the same, but as it is. . . . Of course, there is no God, but if there were, even *He* wouldn't love my neighbor.

We have, then, two cultures in America: the Catholic, which concentrates on the eternal, and the communal, which knows only the temporal. Each encompasses only a *part* of man; as a result, each is a culture of the unreal, the truncated. Central to the Catholic's error is his timid fear of sex, and central to the communal is a denial of God. Sex, I repeat, has its difficulties, difficulties accentuated by the very attractiveness of venereal pleasure. God, too, provides us with difficulties, one of them being our responsibility for our actions. While Catholic writing is a wrestling match between man and God, communal writing is a wrestling match between a man and a woman (though lately it appears that any number and combination can play).

Sex in non-Catholic writing has actually become a literary convention. In fact, sex has become an advertising convention, a movie convention, and a social convention. So permeated is the American culture with sex, sex rational, sex irrational, sex heterosexual, sex homosexual, sex incestuous, that we are finally on the verge of the postsexual age.

Spirituality in Catholic writing has just about always been a literary convention. Inevitably, whenever we pick up something Catholic, we know we will soon hear the rattle of rosary beads, the lisping of some child's confession, the voice of the kindly old priest coaxing the local millionaire to build the gymnasium, the fluttering of young lovers on their way to benediction, and the tinkling voice of Loretta Young as she opens the door of a nunnery. There are some who say we live in a post-Christian age.

What is needed is a coming together. We suffer culturally; others suffer spiritually. We carry the host; others carry the day.

But Catholics can't help society unless they are willing (they should be eager) to leave the soft security of their ghetto and enter into the fire of life.

10

THE FIRE OF LIFE

COURAGE is the measuring rod of all virtue. There is no merit in a man's being prudent if he has never been tempted to be rash. Chastity is a limp thing if one has never felt the rush of passion. Faith counts for little if there has never been some nagging doubt. Obedience loses significance if it is merely reflex action. And charity is as ashes if never challenged by an unkind thought.

Courage is not conceit. It is not founded on one's assurance that one can do no wrong, that one can outthink another, that one is more clever, stronger, more reserved, or even more humble than another. Courage is not blind stubbornness; nor is it rashness. Courage does not proceed from ignorance, but rather can flow only from full knowledge. Courage is not a presumption of God; it is a *reliance* on God.

When we believe in God, we can rely on God's love, assuming, of course, that we not only believe in but also *love* God. Our belief, however, cannot be a vague sort of thing or a variable emotional attachment to some subjective projection of what we would like God to be. Man does not draw up specifications for God; God is the One Who does the specifying. First there is faith in God and God's love, and then comes the courage that marks virtue.

It takes very little courage for me to stand on a street corner and tell the world that I am opposed to communism; I live in America. It would be quite a different thing to repeat my loud remarks on the steps of Lenin's tomb. It is easy for Catholics to say and do many things when they are among their own kind. But what if Catholics were to step out of their community and take on, for example, the question of racial injustice in the South? I don't mean a few tepid and repetitious press releases from the local chancery and I don't mean a summary statement by the American bishops. I mean bishops and priests and laymen joining their fellow human beings in a Southern jail. Is the bishop afraid of losing his dignity or dirtying his hands? Is the priest afraid of what his parishioners will do when he faces them the next Sunday? Is the layman afraid of being conspicuous, of being hurt?

Courage does not rest on certainty. Indeed, courage rests only on uncertainty. It takes little courage to champion a cause sure to win, such as a Democratic victory in Cook County, Illinois, or, contrarily, a cause sure to lose, as when a politically minded Senator opposes the defense budget. Courage is required only when there is risk.

The Catholic Church in America possesses virtue, but it lacks the courage to give meaning to virtue. It possesses truth, but it lacks the courage to bring truth to others. It possesses charity, but it lacks the courage to extend charity to others. It possesses hope, but it lacks the courage to give hope to others. There was once a time when the Church had the courage to go out to the barbarians; today it stands on its own threshold, never daring so much as to put its foot on barbarian land. The Church today lives in the midst of the barbarians, but not with them.

We have the same love of God and of our neighbor we once had. We have the same faith and hope and charity. Why, then, can't we win the day?

We don't have the courage of the early Christians. The single most distinguishing characteristic of the early Christians (during about the first 800 years A.D.) was their willingness to risk death for the faith. They weren't necessarily going out to die for the faith; they were going out to bring the faith to others. For this they chanced privation, abuse, imprisonment, freezing in the north and roasting in the desert, and death. It was to bring the faith to others that they trekked the earth on bleeding feet and fought off the terrors of the vast unknown lands they invaded with nothing more than a cross and a message. But what a cross! What a message! And when civilization broke down under the repeated onslaughts of the barbarians, when Rome was laid waste and total chaos threatened, there was the Church, flung across the Western world like a vast net holding everything together, from the peat bogs in Ireland to the tents on the plains of Asia, from the frozen huts of Scandinavia to the ancient ruins of Rome.

And today? Today we don't go out; we look out. From our comfortable chanceries, our secure rectories, and our mortgaged ranch houses, we stare at the world and shudder. Then we comfort ourselves by huddling closer together as if to forget what we have seen. We love God. We love our neighbor. But from a distance. If for one instant we were to be close to our neighbors, conscience would demand we do something. This is the problem. If we attempt something we may fail. And this we cannot risk.

In the early days Christianity had nothing to lose, so great risks could be taken. The Christian had only his life to lose and only his faith to sustain him. Today we suffer from plenty, particularly in America. We have fantastic tangible wealth in the form of land, churches, schools, colleges, publishing industries, and a thousand other holdings from commercial real estate to corporate stocks and bonds. What if we should lose all this? More significant, however, are the hazards to intangibles. We have finally recovered from the Protestant Reformation and the humiliation it caused us. We are accepted by most of society, and are relieved that the hissing has stopped. We are generally considered decent fellows by our neighbors, some of whom will even vote for us in political elections. Our people are important to industry and commerce; our clerics are members of various government agencies, from atomic energy commissions to civil rights committees. We are accorded full religious and civil liberties. In short, we are respectable.

And we are fat. The rest of the Church looks to America for most of its support. From America comes the money for the missions, money to run the central government in Rome, money to feed and educate the poor, and money to train priests. We are rich and powerful. We have a lot of

weight to throw around. No newspaper dares criticize a
bishop except in the most deferential terms. The entire eth-
ical code group for the movies looks to the Catholics before
it passes on a film. The same is true in politics. No candidate would dare charge his opponent with being a Catholic
(at least publicly, although privately anything goes; but
then, of course, the candidate can deny everything). Tradi-
tionally, at least one Supreme Court justice and one cabinet
member are of the Catholic faith. All this because Catholics
are powerful, *not* because Catholics are good, bad, or indifferent.

The Catholic Church in America is probably the strong-
est single political, social, and economic force in the country. Its bishops and cardinals are deferred to, its clergy
treated with courtesy, its opinions considered—again, not
because the men are good or their views right, but because
the Catholic Church is powerful.

Expressed in vulgar terms, we've got it made. So why
risk all this? And for what?

Only an uncertainty. This is why courage is the mark of
all virtue, the courage to risk all we have for something
uncertain. If it were simple and safe for Catholics to break
out of their ghetto, live with the barbarians, and infuse barbarian society with Christianity, we probably would have
done so before. But there are risks in such an undertaking.
There is little danger to one's *life,* but great danger to one's
easy life, to one's rock-bound certitude, to one's facile solutions; danger that one's hands and mind might get soiled,
that one will argue and lose, that one will be laughed at,
made a fool of, ridiculed, be proved wrong in so much.

Spreading the faith doesn't consist in preaching from Catholic pulpits or in Catholic newspapers or in Catholic schools, which merely shores up our own faith. Spreading the faith consists in going out and *living* the faith in the midst of society. Living the faith doesn't mean passively counting beads at home or unobtrusively attending mass. It does not mean adjusting to hostile circumstances that perpetuate secularism, hedonism, materialism, and all the other isms that grow like weeds everywhere. It does not mean beating one's neighbor over the head with a crucifix or ensnaring him in a clever syllogism. It means *example,* and not in the form of a bowed head and holy mien, not in sanctimonious withdrawal from unpleasant company, not in unctuous words of shallow religiosity. And the first example should consist in the razing of the Catholic ghetto.

We have not just one Catholic ghetto but two, one inside the other. Just as the Church as a whole fears ordinary society, so too the inner ghetto fears the outer. In the very center, the supposed heart of the ghetto, is the corporate structure, which feels itself to be the only true Church. It is bounded on all sides by the laity, who constitute the outer ghetto. The laity are thought to be not very different from the rest of ordinary society in that they are not really *in* the Church (if they were, they would take the vows). Laymen are untrustworthy, secretly secular, and anticlerical (which means anti-Catholic).

The problem is one of numbers and strategic deployment. There are far too few priests. Should they be deployed in ghetto number 1, ghetto number 2, or outside of both?

The pleasantest would be to deploy them in ghetto num-

ber 1, where they could administer the dioceses, run the
parochial school systems, run all the bishops' agencies, edit
the diocesan newspapers, publish devotional tracts and pious magazines, administer and teach in the colleges, and
educate future priests who, when they grew up, could in
turn administer the dioceses, et cetera, et cetera. However,
being celibate, priests produce no children, and in very
short order—if they didn't do something drastic—everything would come to a halt.

But they *do* take drastic action. They enter ghetto number 2 and live openly among the laity. They have their
parishes and schools where good Catholic boys and girls are
scrutinized for vocations. Indoctrination marks the education system, and every child is trained to believe that the
highest—indeed, the only honorable—vocation is the
priesthood or sisterhood. Anything less is both a dereliction
and a proof that one is obstinately refusing God's grace.

This recruiting method appears to be quite effective because a surprising number of boys (they are not even young
men yet) begin the long climb up to near-sanctification,
that is, the priesthood. Of course, close to nine out of ten
who start never finish, which should make those responsible
for the recruiting policies take a second look at their handi-
work. The modern excuse for this awful inefficiency is that
"the boy lacked a vocation." This is not true at all. He
always had a vocation, but not the one that anxious clerics
and anxious parents selected for him.

When the priests* are not trying to replenish ghetto

---

* Equally guilty are the nuns who handle many of the children during
their most delicate years as if they were fallen, utterly fallen, angels.
The sisters are not part of the power structure, but they are part of the
corporate structure, somewhat like junior clerks in a large corporation.

number 1, they are busy preserving and protecting ghetto number 2 from the rest of society. They get their directives from the bishops, and are to obey the word sent down to the last jot and tittle. Unfortunately, at least from the bishops' point of view, exposure to ghetto number 2 can also expose the priest to the rest of society. This unsolicited experience sometimes has the extraordinary effect of forcing the priest to reorder his indoctrinated views on fallen man, which can lead to a revolution in his thinking. If this is not well-hidden, it often results in a transfer to the chancery or some vapid publication directed toward Catholic youth.

Imagine if a priest affiliated with a Protestant or Jewish group for some purpose—or rather, if he tried, because he couldn't without prior permission from the bishop. And too often the bishop must have a guarantee of the sterile nature of the venture before he will allow even the most tenuous affiliation. More likely, he will set up a Catholic counterpart to the proposed project and place the originating priest in charge (he is interested, and also this ploy returns him to the bosom of ghetto number 1 where he can't cause any further mischief). The counterpart will get a set of initials and laymen will be urged to support it both personally and financially. Once organized, the counterpart will just *be;* it won't do anything besides show how we, too, are aware of the needs of modern man. If the bishop is lucky, he will get the thing into the Community Chest so that non-Catholics can help pay the bills.

No. The priest can go only to the second ghetto and no farther. While he lives in the community, the priest must carry his ghetto with him.

But the world is changing. Old methods of peaceful co-existence simply won't work any longer. Separate but equal facilities serve neither Catholics nor the rest of society; they merely isolate the Catholic. Separation prevents the Church from providing the leaven modern society desperately needs if it is to lift itself out of its spiritual and social swamp.

Lately there has been talk of opening a few doors in the second ghetto. It is just talk, however; the corporate structure is still too unsure of the laity actually to turn the key.

The whole business is really ridiculous. The clergy don't trust or respect the laity, the laity resent the clergy, and the rest of society, despite improved relations, looks warily at both of us, just as we think of them as "all those others," renegades, enemies. This is utter nonsense, but we won't do away with it unless we stop being so frightened of one another. We must all learn to trust each other—and God, for that matter.

The layman resents the cleric because he suspects a secret conceit in him that matches the ancient Pharisee's. The layman feels "put upon," a second-class citizen, when he thinks of the clergy. But the layman has his conceit, too, when he looks down on non-Catholics. He has it made, salvation secure in his hip pocket. Besides, he belongs to the biggest and most exclusive religious club in the world. He's got it, going back 2000 years, and will have it for 2000 or 100,000,000 years ahead.

"The others," the rest of society, recall the Spanish Inquisition, the Galileo fiasco, the immoralities of the Renaissance Church, the history of excommunications and interdicts, the religious wars, the persecutions, and the political machinations of Talleyrand, Richelieu, and the Borgias. They read about the persecution of Protestants in Spain and Latin America, papal infallibility, and the Church's obstinate stand on so many pressing social issues. They see a vast structure, a monolith that has unlimited power on the top and abject servitude on the bottom. What a horrible picture! Would you trust such an organization? Wouldn't you wonder a bit?

We fear each other because we don't know each other. Over the centuries Catholics and Protestants have been total strangers. And in Catholic terms, does the layman really know the priest? Does the priest really know the layman?

The failure to know "the other" cuts both ways, but in candor I think that the Church has been more derelict, by failing to relate to changing society. We believe we hold a body of truth, and we would Christianize society as well as save souls. It is all of a piece: you don't save souls by bludgeoning the mind; you do it by Christian example, living a life based on the truths you possess. And these truths must be expressed not as they proved viable in ancient times but in relation to modern society. We must learn the language of our times before we can speak in authentic Catholic terms.

It is for this reason that we must destroy the Catholic ghetto erected centuries ago; it serves only to preserve what should by now be a dead language.

At this point we must not construct a new ghetto, something more modern and colloquial. That would not serve our present needs, and further, it would too likely curse the

future with an outdated monstrosity similar to our own today. It is imperative that everyone understand the need for
the *end* of separation, the need for the living presence of
Catholicism in the general community.

Without doubt the most difficult task will be razing
what I call ghetto number 1. Regardless of the difficulty, it
must be done and done first, because it is the key to everything else. Bringing down the walls is primarily a matter of
changing attitudes. And the attitude of the majority of the
clergy (especially in the hierarchy) has been fixed for centuries on the contention that they and they alone are fit to
rule, that they and only they have the wisdom and prudence
to control the lives of hundreds of millions of people, not
merely in spiritual matters but in all other areas. Two consequences flow from this: first, the laity are to do what they
are told, with no questions asked; second, the laity, being
susceptible to the slightest moral and cultural disease, must
be insulated against common society.

The first breakdown, then, will have to be of attitudes
which provide the inner ghetto with its *raison d'être*. Nothing can be done until the corporate structure puts aside its
own corporate image and the people in it recognize the rest
of the Church as equal members of the Mystical Body.
Once this self-deception could be gotten away with, but the
world is not so simple any more; it is a complex, demanding
world that won't accept either simple or false solutions. The
time has passed when ignorance was the mark of the laity,
and the time has passed when men would automatically
accept domination and exclusion. Look at Africa; look at

the Negro American. We are brethren of the clergy, distinct, but equal in dignity.

Therefore, the command of yesterday must give way to the counsel of today, the dead heritage of past domination must give way to the sharing of today, and the conceit of history must give way to the humility of today—and tomorrow. There has been scandal and it must cease.

Only when our separated brethren, the clergy, see us laymen as brethren united with them will we be able to reduce the inner ghetto to ashes. And then we will be able to break down the ghetto walls that separate us from the rest of society. Then and only then will we be able to enter fully into the missionary task, set by our Lord, which has but one message to preach: *brethren, love one another.* Love doesn't consist of separation; it doesn't depend on sterile isolation or rest on spiritual conceit. It consists of sharing, the sharing of one's spiritual goods, of one's joys and sorrows, of one's innermost yearnings. It consists of comforting the afflicted, feeding the hungry of spirit, granting sanctuary to the wandering soul, and above all at this time, of listening to the voice of our brethren and speaking in a voice that he can hear and understand.

All this requires great courage because the path to be taken has yet to be laid out. Centuries of clerical tradition cannot be casually dismissed, and centuries of lay inertia cannot be suddenly overcome; centuries of Catholic separation will not end in one brief season.

This entire discussion, with few exceptions, has refrained from specific suggestions regarding institutional changes, for the important reason that we must change our *attitudes* before we can discover the course to be taken. Our efforts at this time should be reflective, not active. We should reflect upon ourselves and our beliefs, prejudices, and fears. But we cannot do so without simultaneously reflecting upon the plight of the world. We must not focus solely upon our needs; indeed, we must consider them less in order to consider the needs of our neighbors more.

And though in time we may find it necessary to modify or even abandon certain practices and institutions that have lost purpose, though the visible structure of the Church may appear slightly or even greatly diminished, though traditional relationships may change to various extents, none of this will make the Church less. Rather it will make the Church more, because the Church will have ended its inward concentration and will have begun its greatest period of expansion, possibly not noticeable to the human eye but certainly perceptible to the human heart.

In Church matters, I am obviously Jeffersonian: the least government is the best government. Protect the essentials, trust in the Holy Ghost, and may God have mercy on our souls. This is precisely the point. The Church has endured for 2000 years, years that have seen its temporal power wax and wane, years that have seen the Church commit the most heinous acts imaginable as well as the most glorious, years that have witnessed the most servile denial of Christ's message as well as the most transcendent martyrdom, years that have offered insult to all and years that have saved the world from damnation. Have we, the little mortals who have represented the Church, accomplished this all on our own? Not we but the promises of Christ have endured.

The quaint superstition that *we* have endured is the rankest presumption.

Similarly, how can we account for the rest of society? Surely we cannot say that our frailty has allowed the Protestants, the Jews, and those who defy definition to continue and even flourish right down to this moment. No. We have had nothing to do with it. Man, whether he is a conceited Catholic or an equally conceited atheist, exists because it is God's will. But it doesn't end there. How can we explain the philosopher who denies God, the sexual offender who practices the basest perversions, the wage earner who cheats his employer, the religious who denies the speciality of the Catholic Church, the Catholic who denies the Jew, the Jew who denies the Christian, the atheist who seeks to destroy Christianity, the ditch digger who refuses to dig, the scholar who twists the evidence, the man who kills his friend, the mother who abandons her children? God, Whose existence so many of us doubt or deny, is the ultimate answer. We endure, we live, we hate, we love, we profane the very name *man,* not because we are men but because God is God. We are what we are and God is what He is. We don't exist in our sin because of ourselves; we do so because God loves us, not because we are good but because He is good.

What an extraordinary business this is! God loves us— not just those who publicly profess allegiance to Rome, but those who deny Rome; not just those who pray the mass, but those who spit on the the saint's relic that marks the altar; not only those who pray to our Lady, but those who accuse her of indescribable foulness; not only the chaste child, but the molester of little girls; not only the scholar who proves God's existence, but the scholar who perverts every formable mind that enters his classroom.

This is what makes us all one: God's love. It is no easy thing to be superior or more praiseworthy; it doesn't shake God's love for us. And so it is that we cannot rest on our laurels or relax in our own conceit. We have been given a task, each of us who are born, to dwell not in splendid separation from our fellow man but in union with all men.

There should be no fear, no hesitancy; rather there should be an urgency to break down the walls of separation. What have we to lose? Nothing, once we fully realize that God loves us all, not just you, but me as well. Is anything else important? Only one thing: that we love one another as children of God rather than as strangers. There really are no hazards to the razing of the Catholic ghetto if only we will trust God and if only we will trust our brethren. Our brethren and we are not necessarily good; that is beside the point. They are loved by God no less than are we, who are so sure of God's love for us and of our love for Him. What conceit to equate God's love with our own sickly imitation! But we are stuck with ourselves just as God is stuck with us—and our brethren.

If there is to be a tomorrow, if we are to enter a new age defined in any terms at all, the terms must be terms of love. We here on our aging earth, beset as we are by mortal anguish, afraid for our souls and our destinies, appalled by the baleful specter of mutual annihilation, obsessed with the cares of the day, can take comfort in the ancient experience of Shadrach, Meshach, and Abednego. Captive in an alien land, and clad only in their ordinary garments, they filled the fiery furnace prepared for them by Nebuchadnezzar with their praise of God. But it wasn't their faith alone that preserved them from death. God, Whose praises they sang, spared them from Nebuchadnezzar's wrath as a wondrous sign of His love. And then Nebuchadnezzar bowed down in worship of God.

Can we do less?

About the Author

EDWARD M. KEATING, publisher and editor-in-chief of *Ramparts* magazine, was born in New York City in 1925. He received an A.B. and LL.B from Stanford University, and has been lawyer, lecturer, businessman and teacher. In 1961 Mr. Keating started *Ramparts* and turned to writing. THE SCANDAL OF SILENCE is his first published book. He lives in Menlo Park, California, with his wife and five children.